Transatlantic Perspectives on the Euro

Transatlantic Perspectives on the Euro

C. RANDALL HENNING
and
PIER CARLO PADOAN

HG
925
.H47
2010
West

European Community Studies Association
Pittsburgh, Pennsylvania

Brookings Institution Press
Washington, D.C.

Transatlantic Perspectives on the Euro may be ordered from:

BROOKINGS INSTITUTION PRESS
1775 Massachusetts Avenue, N.W.
Washington, DC 20036
Tel: 1-800/275-1447 or 202/797-6258
Fax: 202/797-6004
www.brookings.edu

Library of Congress Cataloging-in-Publication data
Henning, C. Randall.
    Transatlantic perspectives on the euro / C. Randall Henning and Pier
Carlo Padoan.
        p.   cm.
Includes bibliographical references and index.
        ISBN 0-8157-3559-6 (pbk.: alk. paper)
    1. Euro. 2. Euro—United States. 3. Monetary policy—European Union
countries. 4. Monetary unions—European Union countries. 5. United
States—Foreign economic relations—European Union countries.
6. European Union countries—Foreign economic relations—United States.
I. Padoan, Pier Carlo, 1950– II. Title.
    HG925.H47 2000   99-050737
    337.4073—dc21   CIP

                        9 8 7 6 5 4 3 2 1

The paper used in this publication meets minimum requirements of the
American National Standard for Information Sciences—
Permanence of Paper for Printed Library Materials: ANSI Z39.48-1984.

Typeset in Palatino

Composition by Linda C. Humphrey

Printed by R. R. Donnelley and Sons
Harrisonburg, Virginia

Contents

Foreword

THE DECISION OF EUROPEAN UNION (EU) leaders to abolish their national currencies and create a new unified European money, the euro, is surely one of the most significant political and economic events of the twentieth century. Economic and Monetary Union (EMU), which began January 1, 1999, has been portrayed by its supporters as a way to lock in the peace and economic prosperity that the EU states have enjoyed over the past five decades while sharing those benefits with the United States. EMU's detractors have argued, however, that economic and political differences among the EU states may turn the single currency into too tight a constraint, with the potential to harm not only the European Union but also its international partners. EMU thus is a compelling topic for this fourth volume in the U.S.-EU Relations Project series of the European Community Studies Association (ECSA).

Given the complexity of the issues at stake in EMU, we were very fortunate to have two of the foremost analysts of monetary integration participate in the ECSA project. C. Randall Henning and Pier Carlo Padoan offer an unusually comprehensive and perceptive pair of analyses of the potentials and pitfalls of EMU in the context of U.S.-EU relations by using the lenses of both economic and political theory and drawing on perspectives from both sides of the Atlantic.

Padoan's appraisal of the international monetary implications of EMU and Henning's assessments of its political and international institutional repercussions demonstrate the fruitfulness of a balanced and nuanced analysis of the claims of both the supporters and detractors of the euro. We believe the final product reflects our efforts at ECSA to engage in serious and sustained dialogue across different communities, between EU and U.S. citizens, and between scholars and practitioners, be they in business or the public sphere. In conjunction with the TransEuropean Policy Studies Association (TEPSA), early drafts of the discussions were presented at workshops in Washington, D.C., and Brussels, Belgium, where participants from a variety of arenas commented on the works. After revisions, the final drafts were presented at the 1999 ECSA Biennial International Conference in Pittsburgh, Pennsylvania. We look forward to seeing the dialogue on EMU continue with the publication of this work.

Generous financial support was provided by the European Commission (Directorate-General for External Relations), our own European Community Studies Association, TEPSA, the Institute for European Politics (Bonn), and the U.S. Mission to Brussels, without which the project would not have been possible. I would like to thank my colleagues on ECSA's 1999 U.S.-EU Relations Project committee, Pierre-Henri Laurent, chair, Leon Hurwitz, and Wolfgang Wessels of TEPSA. This book is being provided to ECSA members as a benefit of their membership.

KATHLEEN R. MCNAMARA
1997–1999 ECSA Executive Committee

Acknowledgments

THE AUTHORS WISH TO ACKNOWLEDGE the people who organized this project and commented on our presentations and manuscripts. They include Leon Hurwitz, Pierre-Henri Laurent, Kathleen McNamara, and Maria Green Cowles from the European Community Studies Association (ECSA), and Wolfgang Wessels, Jacques Vandamme, and Margareta Theelen from the TransEuropean Policy Studies Association (TEPSA).

For oral comments offered on drafts of chapter 1 at meetings convened by ECSA and TEPSA, Henning wishes to thank David M. Andrews, Jonathan Aronson, Johan Baras, Michael Calingaert, Jonathan Davidson, Bernard Delbecque, Joseph Greenwald, Mark Hallerberg, Carl Lankowski, Jean-Victor Louis, Gary Marks, Richard Portes, Klaus Regling, John Richardson, Glenda Rosenthal, Hans-Eckart Scharrer, and Pierre van der Haegen. Those offering written comments separately include Benjamin J. Cohen, Michele Fratiani, Paul R. Masson, Ellen Meade, Bowman Miller, Francesco Papadia, Robert Raymond, Simon Serfaty, and Anne Thomas. Jason Meyers provided valuable research assistance. A number of officials in the United States, Europe, and international organizations agreed to be interviewed for this chapter on a not-for-attribution basis. Their time and insights have been indispensable.

For comments and suggestions that improved chapter 2, Padoan would like to acknowledge David M. Andrews, Jonathan Aronson, Samuel Barnes, Peter Bekx, Maria Green Cowles, John Greenwald, Mark Hallerberg, Randall Henning, Leon Hurwitz, Gary Marks, Pierre-Henri Laurent, Richard Portes, John Richardson, Glenda Rosenthal, Alberta Sbragia, Hans-Eckart Scharrer, and Wolfgang Wessels. Both authors want to emphasize that none of these people shares responsibility for any shortcomings that might remain in this study.

At the Brookings Institution Press, we would like to acknowledge the guidance of Robert Faherty, director, and the editorial assistance of Vicky Macintyre.

Transatlantic
Perspectives on
the Euro

Introduction

EUROPE'S MONETARY UNION, launched on January 1, 1999, defines a new epoch in monetary history. Various commentators have called the Economic and Monetary Union (EMU) the most important transformation of the international monetary system since the transition to flexible exchange rates in the early 1970s, the Bretton Woods conference of 1944, the replacement of the pound sterling by the dollar as the leading currency in the interwar period, and even the consolidation of the gold standard in the nineteenth century. Whatever the description, monetary union has fundamentally changed the structure of international monetary relations.

The creation of the euro, the new currency of the monetary union, raises a host of questions for the United States, the rest of the world, and the external relations of the European Union (EU). How does the formation of the monetary union affect the interests of the international community? Will international monetary cooperation improve or decline with the consolidation of the euro area? How will the health of transatlantic monetary cooperation affect the global community? Will the monetary union reinforce or hinder the ability of the international community to restore financial stability? How must international institutions adapt to the presence of the monetary union? What will be the external posture of the monetary union? How effectively will the euro compete with the U.S. dollar as an international currency?

This volume concentrates on the ramifications of the euro for transatlantic relations. It asks, fundamentally, whether monetary union will lead to cooperation or rivalry between the United States and Europe. We approach this question by examining the political, economic, and institutional interests of these two principal actors. U.S. concerns are treated by C. Randall Henning in chapter 1 and European concerns by Pier Carlo Padoan in chapter 2.

Henning opens his discussion with a review of selected academic commentary and official U.S. statements about Europe's monetary union. He then analyzes the cross-cutting effects of monetary union on the interests of the United States. He also examines the external monetary policymaking machinery and international representation of the euro area, specifically, in the meetings of finance ministers and central bank governors of the Group of Seven (finance G-7) and the International Monetary Fund (IMF).

Henning is sympathetic to European integration in general, supportive of the monetary union in particular, and persuaded of the importance of international cooperation. But he does not intend to prejudge debate about the future course of the monetary union, its impact on the interests of non-Europeans, or the organization of international cooperation under the euro, and examines alternative views in his portion of the study.

The euro's impact on the interests of the international community, Henning finds, depends on further developments within the European Union. If the European Union provides stability to Central and Eastern Europe, undertakes economic policy reforms, and develops the institutions for external monetary policymaking, then the monetary union will have beneficial effects on the rest of the world, the United States in particular. If the European Union is unable to build upon the monetary union in these ways, the euro's impact outside Europe will not necessarily be favorable.

Since substantial ambiguity remains concerning European mechanisms for external monetary policymaking and representation, Henning contends, the European Union has more work to do in this regard. Clarification and delegation of responsibility for negotiating international monetary agreements with the United States and Japan is particularly important. Countries outside of Europe have an interest, moreover, in further movement within the European Union toward transparent decisionmaking and qualified majority voting. Finally, the United States and Europe should avoid official competition over the international use of their currencies. Liberalization of national capital markets and removal of barriers to investment and financial services within the European Union would be more appropriate and mutually beneficial forms of competition with the United States.

In his analysis, Padoan takes up the question of what role the euro might play as a global currency, a factor crucial to the potential EU-U.S. relationship that Henning has laid out. To answer this question, Padoan examines the factors that might make the euro an attractive currency for investors and economic actors outside the EU area and considers the possible scenarios for euro appreciation or depreciation.

In his appraisal of the euro's potential as a global currency, Padoan begins with the assumption that multiple equilibria in the international financial system are present and anchored in "currency regions" and that there will be a transition phase between a "low" (regional) and a "high" (global) equilibrium. The transition, he notes, will be a function of policy options followed by EMU authorities, particularly EMU's exchange rate policy and its attractiveness for non-EMU countries.

Padoan advocates policies that would focus on long-term stability over an "active" exchange rate policy; such policies would encourage the formation of a currency region that extends beyond the boundaries of the actual currency union. Although the dollar is likely to remain the dominant currency in the short run, Padoan argues that over the long term the euro may well rival the greenback, at which point it will be in the interest of both European and American policymakers to focus on cooperative efforts at stabilizing bilateral rates and ensuring continued economic prosperity.

Padoan discusses not only economic policy options but also the composition of EMU, emphasizing the relationship between the evolution of the exchange rate of the euro and European growth. The net benefit of EMU, he suggests, will increase with the number of members, the size of the EU's gross domestic product (GDP), degree of internal market integration, and monetary and financial convergence. In this regard, he considers several scenarios in which EMU might act as an endogenous currency area for countries that are likely to become part of the euro region, namely, those in Central and Eastern Europe and the Mediterranean. He also discusses the possible impact of instability in the euro-dollar relationship on Latin America.

The euro and dollar are now competing and will continue to compete as international currencies in the marketplace. That competition underscores the need for official cooperation across the Atlantic. Without cooperation between U.S. and European authorities, the risks of monetary and financial instability would be high. With cooperation, the United States and Europe can foster more efficient macroeconomic management and exchange rate stability and improve the functioning of international financial institutions.

1

U.S.-EU Relations after the Inception of the Monetary Union: Cooperation or Rivalry?

C. Randall Henning

AMERICANS HOLD MULTIPLE and conflicting views about the inception of the euro, its effects on their interests, and the prospects for international cooperation. Government officials declare conditional support for monetary union, but their reservations sometimes speak as loudly as their endorsements. The United States and the rest of the world would thus benefit from a balanced, comprehensive analysis of the costs and benefits stemming from the monetary union.

After presenting selected academic and official views of the euro, this chapter offers a preliminary analysis of those costs and benefits. It then elaborates on the adaptation of European institutions for making external monetary policy and of international institutions such as the finance G-7 and International Monetary Fund (IMF). Policymaking institutions in the United States will also have a critical bearing on the future of transatlantic monetary cooperation. Those have been examined extensively elsewhere, however, and the more serious questions at the moment revolve around the European institutions.[1]

---

1. On American external monetary policymaking, see, among others, Destler and Henning (1989); Henning (1994, 1999).

American Views on Monetary Union

Until a year or two before the creation of the euro area, most American opinion leaders tended to perceive European integration to be five to ten years behind its actual progress. The abandonment of previous efforts, the 1992–93 European currency crises, and squabbling among European governments over convergence led most Americans to expect the Maastricht objective to meet the same fate as the Werner plan. Greater exposure to British media and analysis than to continental media reinforced this assessment. Although among the few to appreciate the political momentum behind the Maastricht Treaty, even many specialists in European integration were reserved in their predictions that monetary union would in fact happen. Not until policy convergence and consensus on broad membership in the monetary union became clear did most Americans finally recognize that the euro would be created at the beginning of 1999.

Academic Commentary

Academic commentary on European integration can be grouped into positive-sum and zero-sum analyses. Zero-sum thinkers, a group that includes the neorealist analysts of international relations, emphasize calculations of relative power and thus argue that a successful monetary union will harm U.S. interests. Most American economists are of the positive-sum persuasion, arguing that a smoothly functioning monetary union would create the same benefits for American firms and investors that it would provide for Europeans. At the same time, American economists tend to doubt that monetary union will in fact be successful. If one polled the annual meeting of the American Economic Association, an overwhelming majority would probably respond that monetary union will be bad for Europe. By extension, through positive-sum thinking, it must be also be bad, not good, for the United States.

American economists are guided in this assessment principally by the theory of optimum currency areas. This theory, originating in the 1960s from Robert A. Mundell, Ronald I. McKinnon, Peter B. Kenen, and W. Max Corden, among others, identifies the conditions under which a geographic area should share a single currency or, put another way, should sacrifice the exchange rate as an instrument for adjusting payments imbalances.[2] In applying the theory to Europe, most American economists find that labor mobility, real wage flexibility, and fiscal transfers are insufficient to conclude that the euro-11 is an optimum currency area. However, Mundell and Kenen disagree with these applications and support the monetary union, although for different reasons.

Among the sharpest critics of Economic and Monetary Union (EMU) is MIT economics professor Rudi Dornbusch:

> So EMU has gone from being an improbable and bad idea to a bad idea that is about to come true. . . . The struggle to achieve monetary union under the Maastricht formula may be remembered as one of the more useless battles in European history. The costs of getting there are large, the economic benefits minimal, and the prospects for disappointment major.[3]

"The most serious criticism of EMU," Dornbusch adds, "is that by abandoning exchange rate adjustments it transfers to the labor market the task of adjusting for competitiveness and relative prices. . . . Forcing adjustment into the labor market, the European market with the poorest performance, is bound to fail. . . . Competitive labor markets is the answer, but that is a dirty word in social-welfare Europe."[4] "If there was ever a bad idea," he concludes, "EMU is it."[5]

Former chairman of the Council of Economic Advisers Martin Feldstein has also been a persistent critic of the movement toward monetary union in Europe. Its adverse effects on unemployment and inflation, he argues, would "outweigh any gains from facilitating trade and capital flows among the EMU members."[6] Feldstein believes that "the real rationale for EMU is political and not economic." He warns, however, that conflict over the goals and methods of monetary policy, incompatible expectations about the sharing of power within the union, and issues between members and nonmembers will increase

2. Mundell (1961); McKinnon (1963); Kenen (1969); Corden (1972).
3. Dornbusch (1996, p. 113).
4. Dornbusch (1996, p. 120).
5. Dornbusch (1996, p. 124).
6. Feldstein (1997a, p. 60). See also Feldstein (1997b, 1992).

intra-EU conflict rather than foster political union. Feldstein, conducting a political rather than economic analysis, then makes an extraordinary statement:

> Although 50 years of European peace since the end of World War II may augur well for the future, it must be remembered that there were also more than 50 years of peace between the Congress of Vienna and the Franco-Prussian War. Moreover, contrary to the hopes and assumptions of Monnet and other advocates of European integration, the devastating American Civil War shows that a formal political union is no guarantee against an intra-European war. Although it is impossible to know for certain whether these conflicts would lead to war, it is too real a possibility to ignore in weighing the potential effects of EMU and the European political integration that would follow.[7]

Feldstein elaborates on his political reasoning:

> War within Europe itself would be abhorrent but not impossible. The conflicts over economic policies and interference with national sovereignty could reinforce long-standing animosities based on history, nationality, and religion. . . . A critical feature of the EU in general and EMU in particular is that there is no legitimate way for a member to withdraw. . . . But if countries discover that the shift to a single currency is hurting their economies and that the new political arrangements also are not to their liking, some of them will want to leave. The majority may not look kindly on secession, either out of economic self-interest or a more general concern about the stability of the entire union. The American experience with the secession of the South may contain some lessons about the danger of a treaty or constitution that has no exits.[8]

The United States should expect increased conflict within and with Europe, Feldstein contends. Washington could, however, help to prevent those conflicts from escalating "into more serious confronta-

7. Feldstein (1997a, p. 62).
8. Feldstein (1997a, p. 72).

tions." The United States should declare that "it wants its relations with the individual nations of Europe to remain as strong as they are today and should not allow Brussels to intervene between Washington and the national capitals of Europe."[9] Furthermore, he notes, Europe will want to assert itself in transatlantic relations, and the United States will no longer be able to count on Europe as an ally in its relations with third countries. Although such a divergence would have happened in any case after the fall of Soviet communism, Feldstein adds, monetary union will accelerate it.

Some of Feldstein's remarks mischaracterize European history and contain a glaring contradiction: the internal conflict that he so confidently predicts would block the political union that he also fears. Feldstein cannot logically fear them both simultaneously; he must choose one or the other. Moreover, it is simply not credible that Europeans would take up arms against one another in an attempt to achieve their interest rate objectives. It is far easier to reissue one's own currency and leave the monetary union, notwithstanding the absence of any explicit procedure for doing so within the treaties.

Feldstein's argument deserves closer analysis than I can give it here.[10] Suffice it to say that in my view, we can indeed completely dismiss the possibility of European civil war, Feldstein's suggestion in this regard is not a mainstream American concern, and this suggestion should not be allowed to distract American and European attention from the serious transatlantic issues raised by monetary union. Feldstein's opinion that a successful EMU would harm U.S. interests, especially if it led to political union, is shared by some other Americans, but its prevalence should not be overstated.

From a classical realist perspective, Henry A. Kissinger, too, worries that monetary union, whether it fails or succeeds, will undermine transatlantic political cooperation: "The European currency can succeed only in the context of political unification, and "the nature of that political unity will determine the future of North Atlantic cooperation."[11] A confederal

9. Feldstein (1997a).
10. See, for example, Livingston (1998).
11. See Henry A. Kissinger, "A New Union in Europe," *Washington Post*, May 12, 1998, p. A19.

political union, preserving a role for nation states, would preserve Atlantic cooperation, a federal political union would undercut it.

Those analysts that support the single currency project include, as mentioned earlier, Canadian-born Nobel laureate Robert Mundell. If well run, he writes, EMU will be of "enormous benefit" to the international community.

> Members of the EMU will get not just a currency on a par with the dollar and the right to share in international seigniorage but also greater influence in the running of the international monetary system. The rest of the world will get an alternative asset to the dollar to use in international reserves and a new and stable currency that could be used as the focus for stable exchange rates or currency boards. The U.S. will get a needed relief from the eventually debilitating overuse of the dollar as an international currency, a single-currency continent that vastly simplifies trade and investment, and a strong partner in Europe with an equal stake in constructing an international monetary system suitable for the 21st century.[12]

Richard N. Cooper also supports a common currency for Europe, in principle. However, he strongly objects to the design of the monetary union as laid down in the Maastricht Treaty and now being implemented. Jeffrey A. Frankel and C. Fred Bergsten have spoken in support of the monetary union as implemented. And Frankel and Andrew Rose believe that the formation of a currency area can stimulate the fulfillment of the conditions for optimality ex post, and they offer substantial supporting evidence.[13]

Political scientists, particularly those specializing in political economy and European studies, bring another perspective to the debate. David Cameron suggests that the deflationary monetary policies of the

12. See Robert Mundell, "The Case for the Euro—II," *Wall Street Journal*, March 25, 1998, p. A22.

13. See Frankel and Rose (1998). See also Richard N. Cooper's remarks to the conference on the Euro as a Stabilizer in the International Monetary System, sponsored by the Luxembourg Institute for European and International Studies, Luxembourg, December 3–4, 1998; Jeffrey A. Frankel's comments at the same conference; and C. Fred Bergsten, "The Euro Could Be Good for Trans-Atlantic Relations," *International Herald Tribune*, January 4, 1999, p. 8.

European Central Bank (ECB) could well produce a domestic political backlash within member states against the monetary union. Peter Hall and Robert Franzese reinforce Cameron's warning, arguing that a lack of coordination of wage bargaining within the monetary union could cause unemployment to rise. Torben Iversen agrees that intermediate levels of wage bargaining coordination are likely to have deleterious effects on employment. Barry Eichengreen warns that the Stability and Growth Pact could constrain fiscal policy to the point of reducing European growth. Eichengreen and Jeffry Frieden, seeing no clear economic justification for monetary union, conclude that monetary integration was driven mainly by political factors: interstate bargaining, linkage politics, and domestic distributional issues.[14]

Examining monetary unions of the past, Benjamin J. Cohen emphasizes the restrictiveness of conditions for successful currency areas. Meeting the criteria defined by the theory of optimum currency areas, however, is secondary in importance to the survival of monetary unions. The presence of local hegemons and broad institutional linkages, Cohen argues, is primary. David M. Andrews and Thomas D. Willett offer a different reading of Cohen's cases, attributing the survivability of earlier monetary unions to a combination of economic (optimum currency area criteria) and organizational factors. Andrews and Willett thus offer a more optimistic future for the present monetary union in Europe.[15]

The American public is not often polled about attitudes toward the monetary union. The one poll of which I am aware, conducted in February–April 1998, confirms that Americans in general are not well informed about the euro. When asked how much they had heard about the single-currency project, 42.5 percent of respondents reported they had heard nothing at all, and 24.8 percent reported they had heard very little. When asked about the impact on the United States, 23.8 percent expected the effects to be good, 17.7 percent expected the effects to be bad, and 44.6 percent expected that the euro would make no difference.[16]

---

14. See Eichengreen and Frieden (1994); Eichengreen (1996); Cameron (1997); Hall and Franzese (1998); Iversen (1998).

15. Cohen (1994, 1998); Andrews and Willett (1997).

16. Program on International Policy Attitudes (1998, pp. 81–82).

The same poll identified attitudes regarding the impact of European integration on the United States more broadly. If the countries of the European Union acted together, "almost like a single country," 47.2 percent of respondents thought that this would be "mostly good" for the United States, while 41.4 percent thought that this would be "mostly bad." But in response to the statement that integration would enable the European Union to take on a greater share of the burden of keeping peace and that this would be good for the United States, 82.4 percent of respondents said they agreed.[17]

Official Commentary

Historically, the U.S. government has neither opposed nor actively encouraged monetary integration in Europe, but it has accepted without resistance the European Union's progress in this direction. Underlying the official U.S. position is the attitude that European economic integration in general can be encouraged provided that the process does not restrict American access to the European market. That stance was adopted at the outset, during the establishment of the European Coal and Steel Community in the 1950s, and was reiterated many times thereafter. Likewise, American officials adopted the benign view of monetary integration with some reservations about the particular means and mechanisms by which it was being achieved.[18]

During the approach to the Maastricht summit meeting, the currency crisis of 1992–93, and the convergence process through the mid-1990s, the U.S. Department of the Treasury refused to be drawn into the debate over the desirability of monetary union. Despite occasional entreaties from both sides of that debate, Treasury endeavored to maintain a neutral stance: monetary integration was for the Europeans to decide. Two concerns have nonetheless prompted Treasury officials to speak directly to the merits of creating the euro: that the monetary union would be deflationary and that the markets would construe stated neutrality as silent hostility.[19]

17. Program on International Policy Attitudes (1998, pp. 81–82).

18. U.S. officials adopted this benign stance even though transatlantic monetary conflict was a principal motive for closer regional cooperation in Europe. See Henning (1998).

19. Andrews (1998) also provides a survey of the official U.S. position on EMU.

The possible presence of a deflationary bias in the monetary union and an ensuing drag on growth in the United States and the rest of the world was a fairly constant concern of U.S. policymakers throughout the 1990s. Even before the Maastricht Treaty was concluded at the end of 1991, Secretary Nicholas F. Brady, having underestimated the political momentum behind the monetary union, was furious to learn that European central banks would tighten in unison with the German Bundesbank, which in turn was tightening in response to German unification.

The Clinton administration has shared this concern. Lawrence H. Summers, as deputy secretary of the Treasury, explicitly raised the specter of deflation in early 1996.[20] White House, State Department, and Treasury officials reiterated these concerns at the G-7 summit meeting in Lyon in July 1996.[21] Although the pre-union convergence is now completed for most countries, some American policymakers fear that European authorities will not give sufficient attention to deflationary risks.

Nevertheless, Treasury officials did not want to appear hostile to monetary union per se. To prevent their silence from being construed as opposition, they began to speak more directly to the question of monetary union beginning in 1996. In response to a reporter's question about the euro, Secretary Robert E. Rubin reiterated long-standing U.S. policy: "It is in the interest of the United States for Europe to prosper. We've always said we think European unification serves that purpose and therefore it's good for them, it's also good for us."[22] Summers said, "Successful monetary union in Europe would be good for the world and good for America."[23] Nonetheless, these statements veiled a deep-seated suspicion among U.S. officials, grounded in optimum-currency-area reasoning, that the monetary union might well not be "successful."

---

20. Alan Friedman, "U.S. Official Sees Risk of Deflation in Europe," *International Herald Tribune,* January 22, 1996. See also David Wessel, "U.S. Is Mum as Europe Integrates Economies," *Wall Street Journal,* March 3, 1997, p. A1.

21. Reuter News Service, June 26, 28, and 29, 1996.

22. Department of the Treasury, press briefing, September 29, 1996, Block Court Reporting.

23. Reuter News Service, July 9, 1996.

Summers elaborated on the U.S. position in April 1997. Despite a good historical economic record, he observed, Europe now faced a number of economic challenges, the foremost being the high rate of unemployment. "Achieving a political consensus to deal with these problems has proven quite difficult because the necessary reforms go to the heart of the social democratic consensus in Europe." For Summers, the paradox was that "EMU's success depends on finding strategies to address these challenges, but that EMU itself does not directly address them." Summers warned: "If the process surrounding monetary union distracts Europe from some of its economic and structural challenges, then it will carry an opportunity cost in terms of economic growth foregone."[24] He later elaborated on the reforms that he believed to be necessary: measures to increase labor market flexibility, fiscal consolidation, and structural measures such as privatization and deregulation.[25] His warning fell well short of saying that EMU would be good for the United States.

Summers expected the U.S. dollar to remain the primary reserve currency for the "foreseeable future" and thought that any erosion in its position would occur slowly, if at all. Ultimately, the relative position of the dollar would depend more on the American economy and macroeconomic policies ("the fate of the dollar is still largely in our own hands") than on conditions in Europe or Japan. Although he certainly did not rule out "the possibility of adjustments in relative shares and the like," he expected the dollar to be "the world's major currency for a very long time to come," arguing that "if we manage our economy right, I don't think we have anything to fear from the development by others of successful, attractive currencies."[26]

Summers warned the European Union against introversion during

24. Lawrence H. Summers, "EMU: An American View of Europe," remarks delivered at the Euromoney Conference, April 30, 1997. Department of the Treasury press release.

25. U.S. Senate (1997, pp. 6–21); Lawrence H. Summers, "American eyes on EMU," *Financial Times*, October 22, 1997, p. 14.

26. U.S. Senate (1997, p. 18). See also *Financial Times*, May 1 and October 22, 1997. Summers observed that EMU would affect Europe's position in the global monetary system and international forums such as the G-7 and international financial institutions. These were not questions that needed to be addressed immediately, however, he said. But Europe should prepare itself for a "constructive role on the world stage." Summers, "EMU: An American View of Europe."

the introduction of the monetary union. It was particularly important that European Union maintain the process of eastward enlargement, "an ambitious undertaking and one which the U.S. government hopes will succeed," and continue to open its markets to the global economy.[27] "This requires a strong Europe with a decision making process that permits quick and effective action on an international stage. And it requires that Europe not be overly constrained by protracted domestic preoccupation with the political and economic dimensions of building the architecture and refining the plumbing of monetary union."[28]

Although officials of the Federal Reserve have addressed the subject infrequently, in those rare instances they have supported this basic policy position. When asked in a congressional hearing about monetary union, Chairman Alan Greenspan responded:

> To the extent that it enhances Europe's ability to become an effective world competitor, it's going to help us, not hinder us, because what all of the post–World War II evidence—not to mention earlier, prewar evidence—clearly suggests is that the greater the real growth in trade, the greater the ability of globalization and integration of the various major elements within the international system, the better it is for everybody.[29]

William McDonough, president of New York Federal Reserve Bank, added another dimension to this analysis in October 1998, arguing

27. Summers, "EMU: An American View of Europe," reflecting the views of the State Department. See also Strobe Talbott, "The U.S., the EU, and Our Common Challenges," speech to the conference "Bridging the Atlantic," U.S. Department of State, Washington, D.C. (May 6, 1997); and the analysis in Andrews (1998, pp. 1–11).

28. Later, before hearings of the Senate Budget Committee, Summers put a happier face on U.S. policy: "The cornerstone of American foreign policy for the last 50 years has been support for European integration through the European Coal and Steel Community, to the development of the Common Market, to the development of the single market, and now Europe moves ahead towards monetary union. It is a matter that we watch with great interest." He continued, "The United States has a strong economic and security interest in a stable and prosperous Europe. . . . [I]f EMU works for Europe it will work for the United States. The more the single currency helps Europe develop a robust and healthy economy that is open to world markets, the more welcome the project will be." U.S. Senate (1997, pp. 6–21). See also Summers, "American Eyes on EMU"; and Timothy F. Geithner, then assistant secretary, "The EMU, the United States, and the World Economy," speech to a conference of the Konrad Adenauer-Stiftung and Aspen Institute, Washington, D.C. (May 7, 1998)

29. Senate Banking Committee, July 23, 1997.

that fiscal discipline and competitiveness in Europe will increase market discipline on U.S. fiscal policies as well. In contrast to Treasury's conditional endorsement, McDonough saw EMU as "an unqualified good" for the United States, because it will boost Europe's economy and foster political unity.[30]

In the wake of the financial crisis that began in Asia in 1997, U.S. policymakers stressed that Europe should contribute to current account adjustment. As Vice President Al Gore commented in November 1998, "We hope the EU sees the advent of EMU as an opportunity to press ahead with long-needed structural reforms—and more broadly—to ensure that their policies support strong growth in domestic demand, so that Europe, too, can assist in the Asian recovery and can stand with the United States as a bulwark of global stability."[31] Taking a similar position, Secretary of Commerce William M. Daley, Deputy Secretary Summers, and U.S. Trade Representative Charlene Barshefsky warned that domestic protectionist pressure could rise if the United States accepted a disproportionate share of the exports of crisis-stricken countries.[32]

Amplifying these pronouncements, Assistant Secretary of the Treasury for International Affairs Edwin M. Truman inveighed against the "persistent low levels of domestic European investment" and "Europe's reliance on export-led growth."[33] Changes in policies and regulations that gave more flexibility to the markets for labor, goods, and capital, and the advancement of privatization programs, among other measures, would boost internal investment, he remarked. Not only would these measures stimulate growth and employment within Europe; they would also shift the savings-investment balance

30. *Bloomberg News,* October 26, 1998. For a particularly thoughtful analysis from the Federal Reserve, see Meyer (1999).

31. Al Gore, remarks to the Fourth Annual Transatlantic Business Dialogue, Charlotte, N.C. (November 6, 1998). The vice president reminded his audience of the American government's historical support for European integration and said that it was important for EMU to succeed.

32. See William M. Daley, remarks to the Fourth Annual Transatlantic Business Dialogue, Charlotte, N.C. (November 6, 1998); Lawrence H. Summers, "Transatlantic Implications of the Euro and Global Financial Stability," remarks to the Transatlantic Business Dialogue (November 6, 1998).

33. Edwin M. Truman, "The Single Currency and Europe's Role in the World Economy," remarks to the World Affairs Council, Treasury Department press release, April 6, 1999.

of the euro area, reducing net capital outflows, placing upward pressure on the euro, and reducing the current account surplus of the monetary union.

Notwithstanding these concerns, on January 4, 1999, the first business day after the introduction of the euro, President Bill Clinton reiterated the basic, supportive position of his administration. "A successful economic union that contributes to a dynamic Europe is clearly in our long-term interests," he stated. "The United States has long been an advocate for European integration, and we admire the steady progress that Europe has demonstrated in taking the often difficult budget decisions that make this union possible." Secretary Rubin also stressed the benefits of the monetary union to the United States. Possibly anticipating an appreciation of the euro against the dollar, he added, "I have no doubt markets will fluctuate as they always do; that is not where our focus needs to be."[34]

In sum, U.S. policy is not hostile toward the monetary union. It is distinctly positive-sum in orientation and, at the rhetorical level, certainly supportive. But many officials remain highly skeptical that Europe will be able to muster the reforms to make its economy more flexible and dynamic, create growth and employment, and thus benefit the international community.

American Interests

American interests in monetary union are of a political, economic, and institutional nature. Each of these categories contains both positive- and zero-sum considerations to some degree. They are discussed next, along with those factors on which a mutually beneficial outcome depends.

Political Interests

European monetary union engages the political interests of the United States in at least three (related) ways: (1) it gives impetus to internal economic reforms undertaken in anticipation of enlargement of EU membership; (2) it promotes political integration of the European

---

34. John Authers, "U.S. not fazed by euro's gains," *Financial Times*, January 5, 1999, p. 2.

Union; and (3) it has an impact on Central and Eastern Europe. The next enlargement of EU membership is getting off to a slow start. However, that process would almost certainly be even slower, if not stagnant, without monetary union. Recrimination over the failure to introduce the euro would have raised barriers to agreement on enlargement among the existing member states. Member states know that to enlarge successfully they must reform several of the EU's policies and institutions. In particular, the Common Agricultural Policy and the structural funds in the Community budget must be overhauled. Enlargement is also forcing a further reexamination of Common Foreign and Security Policy. If successful, these policy reviews will probably benefit the United States and transatlantic and multilateral economic relations.

It has often been said that the euro is the monetary means to political integration in Western Europe. The monetary union provides a number of incentives for member states to cooperate in other economic areas such as fiscal and financial policies. Many have argued that the monetary union is better managed under a political union than under a relatively loose collection of member states. Political integration can take the specific form of institutional change, necessitated by the prospect of enlargement and centering on questions such as majority voting and the prerogatives of large and small states.

Through greater political integration in Western Europe, combined with economic deepening, the promise of membership in the EU, and actual membership, the consolidation of the monetary union contributes to economic and political stability in Central and Eastern Europe. A robust and dynamic European Union substantially reduces the likelihood that new U.S. commitments under the enlarged North Atlantic Treaty Organization (NATO) will be tested. Euro-optimism underpins the EU's leading role in the postwar reconstruction of Kosovo. If the monetary union were to fail, Central and Eastern Europe would probably be considerably less stable than in the presence of even a modestly successful EMU. As a consequence, U.S. manpower and resource commitments would have to be correspondingly greater. This geopolitical consideration is profoundly important for U.S. foreign policy.

Economic Interests

As American policymakers recognize, the primary U.S. economic interest revolves around the question of whether the European economy will be dynamic and vigorous or slow-growing. Over the short term, the answer depends on the macroeconomic policies of the euro area. Over the long term, it depends on whether Europe will pursue a substantial list of economic policy reforms to achieve greater labor market flexibility, deregulation, privatization, and fiscal consolidation, including resolution of unfunded pension liabilities. A second major concern is the impact of the euro on the international role of the dollar. A third American interest involves potential constraints on the financing of current account deficits, which could arise if a substantial portion of investors around the world shifted out of dollar and into euro assets.

GROWTH AND STRUCTURAL REFORM. The Stability and Growth Pact establishes tough rules for fiscal policy, backed by sanctions at the discretion of the Council of Ministers. Some analysts expected the fiscal strictures of this pact to be widely violated, a forecast thought to be reinforced by the political dominance of Social Democratic governments over the euro area.[35] Some other analysts forecast that the guidelines would be upheld, but to the detriment of European growth.[36] Preliminary indications suggest, however, that the fiscal rules will be upheld and that reasonable growth will be sustained at least during the first eighteen months of the monetary union. In the expectation that governments would adhere to the Stability and Growth Pact, the European Central Bank and its member national central banks reduced interest rates in December 1998. The coordinated rate cut effectively established 3.0 percent as the ECB intervention rate for the advent of the monetary union. In response to reports of weakening growth in early 1999, particularly in Germany, the ECB reduced interest rates to 2.5 percent in April 1999. Although euro-area growth was nonetheless expected to decline from 3.0 percent in 1998, the euro-11 economy was

---

35. See, for example, Bergsten (1997a; 1997b, p. 86).
36. Eichengreen (1996); de Grauwe (1997, pp. 206–08).

projected to grow by 2.0–2.2 percent in 1999 and accelerate to 2.6–2.9 in 2000.[37]

For the moment, at least, the euro area is effectively pursuing, in the words of French Finance Minister Dominique Strauss-Kahn, the "Clinton-Greenspan" rather than the "Reagan-Volcker" mix of fiscal and monetary policies.[38] Because of its impact on the current account through the exchange rate, the policy mix has important ramifications for the foreign partners of the monetary union. In a nutshell, the tight-fiscal/relaxed-monetary mix ("Clinton-Greenspan") will raise demand in the external sector in relation to the domestic sector of the economy, compared with the relaxed-fiscal/tight-monetary mix ("Reagan-Volcker"). Ceteris paribus, the euro area will thus contribute less to the global current account adjustment in the wake of the global financial crisis than if it embarked on a fiscal spending spree and tightened monetary policy. The implicit bargain between the governments of member states and the ECB underpinning the policy mix, however, is vulnerable to changing political and economic circumstances.[39]

During the winter of 1999, the Clinton administration and Federal Reserve Board Chairman Greenspan publicly advocated European measures to stimulate domestic demand in the euro area and were apparently temporarily mollified by the ECB's interest rate cut of April.[40] U.S. officials nonetheless faced a dilemma: while easing monetary policy stimulated demand, the cut also further weakened the euro against the dollar, with at best ambiguous effects on the current account balance. A fiscal expansion in the euro area would have the desired impact on the current account balances in the short to medium term. American policymakers pressed European governments to undertake fiscal stimuli during several previous episodes of transatlantic macro-

37. These are the ranges of estimates provided by the European Commission, International Monetary Fund, and Organization for Economic Cooperation and Development as of mid-1999. See *Financial Times*, May 28, 1999, survey 4.

38. Dominique Strauss-Kahn, remarks to the fiftieth anniversary of the Centre for Economic Policy Research, London (November 9, 1998).

39. See, for example, John Blitz, "Budget target relaxation 'wrong'," *Financial Times*, May 28, 1999, p. 3.

40. Gerard Baker, "US tires of carrying burden of world growth," *Financial Times*, February 19, 1999, p. 4. See also Baker, "US calls for Europe to aid world growth," *Financial Times*, February 25, 1999, p. 5.

economic conflict, such as the periods 1977–78 and 1985–87.[41] Under current conditions, however, such a stimulus would probably violate the Stability and Growth Pact and threaten to reverse the remarkable improvement in fiscal deficit and debt positions achieved during the pre-euro convergence process. Any sustained increase in European fiscal deficits would worsen an already formidable fiscal challenge for Europe in the coming decades and possibly increase American borrowing costs as well over the long term.

Structural reform would be the way out of this dilemma. Substantial reforms of the markets for labor, capital, goods, and services could stimulate investment and shift the savings-investment balance, capital flows, and the exchange rate of the euro area, supporting, rather than depressing, growth in the rest of the world. The macroeconomic dilemma thus explains the administration's emphasis on structural measures.[42] Although structural reforms usually take a long period of time to implement, particularly in comparison with the macroeconomic instruments, a credible commitment to substantial reforms might affect investment behavior and financial markets over a shorter period of time.

Some analysts argue that EU member states are more likely to slide backward rather than move forward on economic reforms. High rates of unemployment and social democratic political dominance predispose governments toward maintaining, rather than dismantling, the social protections built into the welfare state and continental capitalism. On the other hand, the monetary union itself could well change the political economy of policy reform. Governments can now credibly argue that their macroeconomic hands are tied and that the burden of adjustment rests mainly with private actors. Knowing that exchange rate policy vis à vis other members of the union can no longer reverse the deleterious effects on competitiveness of high wage and price increases, firms and unions should act with greater discipline. Furthermore, national governments can redirect the political capital that had been devoted to securing monetary union to economic reform. Structural reform in Europe can by no means be written off.

41. See Putnam and Henning (1989) and Destler and Henning (1989), respectively.
42. See, for example, Truman's 1999 speech.

INTERNATIONAL ROLES OF THE DOLLAR AND THE EURO. U.S. economic interests will also be affected by the roles that the dollar and euro come to play in the international monetary system. Since the 1930s the dollar has been more important than any other currency as a store of value, medium of exchange, and unit of account for private and official purposes. As of 1995, the dollar accounted for 61.5 percent of official foreign exchange reserves, 76.8 percent of international bank loans, 39.5 percent of international bond issues, and 44.3 percent of eurocurrency deposits. The second currency, the deutsche mark, constituted 14.2 percent of official reserves, 4.9 percent of bank loans, 15.5 percent of bond issues, and 16.9 percent of eurocurrency deposits.[43] But the role of this and of other European currencies was inflated by cross-holdings among European countries. Excluding these intra-European assets would increase even further the measured, mid-1990s benchmark for the role of the dollar.

That role remains considerably larger than the economic size of the United States and its importance in international trade would seem to justify, while the roles of other currencies remain considerably smaller than their shares of gross domestic product (GDP).[44] Monetary union will change the official and private use of currencies substantially. Because the role of the individual European currencies has lagged behind European growth and trade and because the creation of the European monetary bloc will precipitate a quantum shift in the international system, says one group of analysts, the euro will displace the dollar for a large share of its international role.[45] Another group of analysts downplays the prospects for the euro, emphasizing inertia and network externalities in the international use of currencies, while in some cases acknowledging that the new European currency has considerable potential in the long run.[46]

Whichever scenario proves to be most accurate, it will have far-

43. Bank for International Settlements (BIS) (1996).
44. See, for example, Ilzkovitz (1996).
45. European Commission (1990, 1997); Gros and Thygesen (1992); Thygesen and ECU Institute (1995); Ilzkovitz (1996); Bergsten (1997a, 1997b); Portes and Rey (1998).
46. Bénassy, Italianer, and Pisani-Ferry (1994); Johnson (1994); Frankel (1995); Bénassy-Quéré (1996); Kenen (1995); Eichengreen and Frankel (1996); Hartman (1996); Cohen (1997); Masson and Turtelboom (1997); Cooper (1999); Fratianni, Hauskrecht, and Maccario (1999).

reaching consequences for the operation of international markets and the trade and investment flows of the United States. If the euro were to close one-half of the gap between it and the dollar as a currency of denomination of private international financial assets, for example, roughly $400 billion in investments would be reallocated from dollar to euro assets. On the official side, about $75 billion in official reserve assets could be similarly reallocated. If the euro were to come to play a role equal to that of the dollar, about $800 billion in private assets and $150 billion in official reserves could be reinvested from dollar to euro assets.[47] Changes in the demand for dollar and euro assets will be at least partly offset by changes in the supply of such assets. Although rough, these numbers nonetheless suggest that such a shift carries substantial stakes for the United States.

Many attributes of the home country or currency union jointly determine the international role that its currency comes to play: economic size, share of global trade, long-term external payments position, international status as creditor or debtor, posture of the authorities, network effects, and size and openness of internal financial markets, among others.[48] Assuming that the present "outs" eventually join the monetary union, the U.S. and euro area will be roughly equal, though not exactly equal, on the fundamental parameters of GDP and share in international trade. The United States is at a disadvantage in the category of current account position and debtor status, but this could be offset by the advantage of incumbency and network effects. Thus the scenario for currency usage that prevails will hinge greatly on the pace and extent of the broadening and deepening of the European financial and capital markets. Just as the British capital markets underpinned the role of the pound sterling in its heyday, and as the American capital market has underpinned the role of the U.S. dollar since the 1930s, the strength and diversity of the European capital market will underpin (or undermine) the role of the euro.

By eliminating exchange rate risk, monetary union itself will do much to integrate the European capital market. The valuation of European government bonds outstanding will rival that of U.S. govern-

47. These estimates are based on 1995 data for the EU15 as a whole. See Henning (1997, pp. 21–25).

48. See, for example, Bergsten (1997a); Frenkel and Goldstein (1999).

ment bonds. This market is growing in relation to that in the United States because beginning in 1999 all euro-area governments are issuing new debt in euro denomination and redenominating outstanding debt. The short-term repurchase market is benefiting from the open-market operations conducted by the euro-area central banking system. The small corporate bond market can be expected to grow fairly quickly.

The broad European capital markets nonetheless remain much smaller than the American market. Stock market capitalization of the euro-11 countries was roughly one-third that of the United States in 1995. Adding the United Kingdom would raise that figure to about one-half. The value of all debt securities outstanding was about $7 trillion among the euro-11 in 1995, compared with $11 trillion in the United States.[49]

Several factors continue to segment European capital markets even after the creation of the euro. First, though the European government bond market is large, it is not dominated by a single issuer such as the U.S. Treasury in the American market. Instead, the market is composed of many issuing governments, the Italian, German, and French being the largest issuers. Default risk has replaced exchange risk. National government bonds carry somewhat different yields and are traded separately. Second, primary dealing in government securities remains at the national level. Third, tax policies, regulatory practices, accounting standards, bankruptcy regimes, and collateral rules continue to segment national markets. Further harmonization of these policies and practices will be necessary before the European market rivals the American financial market.[50] Britain's entry into the monetary union would greatly strengthen the European financial market and enhance the appeal of the euro as the currency of denomination of international assets and liabilities. If European capital markets were unified and the dollar were displaced by the euro, the United States would stand to lose in three principal areas: seigniorage, exchange rate risk, and automatic financing (which is discussed in the next subsection).

49. IMF (1997).
50. See, for example, IMF (1997, annexes II and IV); Centre for European Policy Studies (1998).

Foreign residents probably hold more than a majority of dollar currency in circulation.[51] These holdings represent an interest-free loan to the United States. Taking 60 as the percentage of foreign holdings, the value of the loan amounts to roughly $15 billion to $20 billion per year. This seigniorage is whittled down to the extent that the euro displaces the dollar in these holdings. If the euro equaled the dollar, the seigniorage loss could amount to roughly 0.1 percent of GDP. To this can be added losses associated with the liquidity premium—the extent to which foreign investors in dollar assets create greater liquidity in the U.S. bond market, reducing interest costs—which are about 0.1 percent of GDP as well.[52]

To the extent that foreign actors are willing to hold dollar-denominated claims against the United States in lieu of buying goods and services, American issuers avoid the exchange rate risk that would otherwise attend international borrowing to finance current account deficits. To the extent that American trade and investment are denominated in other currencies, such as the euro, American issuers will incur currency risk. But the importance of such risk and loss of seigniorage is likely to be small in macroeconomic terms for the United States as a whole.

FINANCIAL DISTURBANCES AND POTENTIAL CONSTRAINTS. Potential financial constraints could be considerably more important for the U.S. economy. Foreign acceptance of dollar-denominated American liabilities has rendered credit extension virtually automatic. Assuming that the euro could play, at the most, a role equal to that of the dollar over the long run, roughly 40 percent of international assets will continue to be denominated in dollars. The United States would thus appear to have ample room to finance external deficits by issuing dollar liabilities.

Dangers for the United States could nonetheless arise from the *transition* to a new pattern of currency usage and *subsequent* payments-financing constraints in unusual circumstances. Consider first the transition to the new pattern of currency roles. As Padoan contends, the

51. Porter and Judson (1996); Rogoff (1998).
52. Portes and Rey (1998).

international use of currencies might well be characterized by multiple equilibria. That is, *both* a large role for the dollar with a modest role for the euro *and* a moderate role for the dollar with a roughly equivalent role for the euro could be consistent with a single set of structural conditions. Under these circumstances, the actual choice of equilibrium could be the product of historical accident, simple inertia, market expectations, or beliefs. If the choice is a function of expectations and beliefs, the equilibrium could be unstable.[53]

The *speed* of the shift from one equilibrium to another also carries serious ramifications for the United States. Given the stock of international financial assets in dollars, a rapid shift of even a minority share of these assets could have major consequences for capital flows, the exchange rate, current account balances, and domestic financial markets. Those consequences would be greater if domestic assets on both sides of the Atlantic came into play during a crisis. The United States has a strong interest in the rebalancing of portfolios being smooth and gradual rather than precipitous.

Europe shares this interest but might nonetheless be tempted to encourage the shift into the euro. A greater international role for the euro, compared with the combined roles of the preceding national currencies, is among the prime benefits of a common currency cited by a number of Europeans. Europeans could well seek to capture these perceived advantages for the monetary union, now that the euro is a more strongly competing currency.[54] Possible European actions include campaigning for the use of the euro in official reserve holdings of third countries, encouraging the use of the euro as a nominal anchor outside the European Union, reducing official European holdings of U.S. dollars in reserves, and promoting the euro as an invoicing currency.[55] If unchecked, competition between the United States and European Union in the international use of their currencies could

53. See chapter 2 in this volume; also Alogoskoufis and Portes (1997); Rey (1997).
54. Cohen (1998).
55. Commissioner de Silguy, for example, campaigned for the use of the euro in China. For proposed use of the euro as a nominal anchor outside the European Union, see Emerson (1999) and Emerson and others (1999). The creation of the monetary union reduces the need for the national central banks and the European Central Bank to hold foreign exchange reserves. I estimate excess dollar reserves in Europe to amount to roughly $50 billion to $100 billion (Henning 1997).

interfere with cooperation in areas of far greater economic signifi-cance. It would be particularly damaging and senseless for the Federal Reserve and European Central Bank to bolster the use of their curren-cies by tightening monetary policy or failing to ease when that was de-sirable. Fortunately, as of the first year of the monetary union, the ECB has taken a deliberately neutral posture with respect to the interna-tional role of the euro.[56]

The emergence of a more robust alternative to the dollar than the deutsche mark and yen will render the international environment less forgiving of American policy mistakes, of which there have been many in the postwar period. American policy errors in the future could cause substantially greater portfolio diversification out of dollar assets than in the past. Thus, although the future of the dollar might be primarily in the hands of American authorities, their range of pol-icy options might well become narrower.

In general, the formation of the monetary union and increasing in-ternational role of the euro will not likely constrain U.S. macroeco-nomic policy through any external financing constraint. However, the United States ran a merchandise trade deficit of $248 billion and a cur-rent account deficit of $233 billion in 1998 and was expected to run a merchandise trade deficit well in excess of $300 billion in 1999. The magnitude of these deficits must give pause to even the most compla-cent American economic policymaker. Will U.S. interest rates have to rise over time to perpetuate the inflows of capital that finance these deficits? Could sudden changes in market sentiment cause a drying up of these flows temporarily?

Particularly relevant is American experience in 1987, when at least two-thirds of the huge U.S. current account deficit was financed not by the private markets but by foreign central banks that intervened out of fear of the competitive effects of the appreciation of their cur-rencies against the dollar. If private capital flows into the United States dry up in the future as they did then, European authorities, presiding over a larger and more cohesive monetary union, will not be as vul-nerable to currency appreciation. European authorities would thus

56. European Central Bank (1999, pp. 31–54). The European Monetary Institute had, however, decided to issue large-denomination bills that would be likely to attract un-derground demand. See Rogoff (1998).

not be forced to step into the breach. If they chose to do so, European officials might insist on American policy adjustments as a quid pro quo. U.S. authorities must be cognizant of these possibilities, more so now that the euro financial market has been established and the euro presents a robust alternative to the dollar.

Any such balance of payments constraint would not necessarily diminish U.S. welfare. The Congress, the executive, and the Federal Reserve would resent having their choices circumscribed. However, to the extent that they prevented the U.S. government from pursuing or prolonging policy blunders—such as the overexpansionary monetary policy of the 1970s or the overexpansionary fiscal policy of the 1980s—balance of payments constraints could benefit the United States as a whole. (McDonough, as mentioned above, apparently agrees.)

The euro has already become the second international currency. It will almost surely prove to be a robust competitor to the dollar and could eventually play a role roughly equal to that of the U.S. currency. Whether it will do so depends largely on the pace of the deepening of the European financial market. An increased role for the euro, which implies a decline in that of the dollar, is unlikely to pose major problems for the United States provided that shift is gradual. A precipitous shift could indeed have a negative impact on the U.S. economy. In that case, though, the main concern would be balance of payments financing, extreme exchange rate movements, and higher interest rates, rather than the role of the U.S. currency per se.

Institutional Interests

The monetary union gives rise to a host of European institutional matters—the organization of monetary policymaking and operations, the mechanisms through which fiscal and other economic policies are coordinated among member states, and the institutions through which monetary policy is coordinated with fiscal policy—most of which have been addressed but not fully resolved. It also raises a set of issues that are specifically external in character: the allocation of responsibility for exchange rate and external monetary policy, the process by which exchange rate policy will be set, the international representation of the euro area, and the ratification of international agreements. The EU's solution to each of these institutional questions affects the interests of the United States.

Miles Kahler argues that the international community has an interest in the European Union having transparent decisionmaking and the ability to conclude credible bargains.[57] Requirements for the latter include clear institutional competence, intra-EU coordination, and reasonable efficiency in the reaching of common bargains. To the Kahler list one can add the ability to bargain flexibly—which does not mean weakly—with foreign partners.

The United States has four decades of experience in bargaining with the Community on trade policy. It is fair to say that the formation of the European Community substantially enhanced the negotiating leverage of Western Europe. However, the greater collective power of the Community has not been the main source of frustration for American officials in trade negotiations. Instead, the greater problem for them by far has been the practice of establishing the negotiating position of the Community by a consensus of at least the large member states (despite the treaty provisions subjecting trade matters to qualified majority voting). The internal decision rule, rather than collective power, generated minimalist liberalization offers that could be rendered flexible only with transatlantic brinkmanship (to which U.S. policymaking of course made its own contribution). On several occasions—witness agriculture in the Uruguay Round—deadlock was overcome only when Commission officials exceeded their negotiating mandate to get agreement, for which they secured political support after the fact, a highly conflictual process of intra-EU negotiation. While this pattern of bargaining nonetheless allowed regional and multilateral trade liberalization to progress over the decades, it would be disastrous in the monetary and financial field, where the markets are so much more sensitive to policy conflict and new information.

Security cooperation provides a second analogue. The United States has acceded in principle to use by the Western European Union (WEU), the provisional embodiment of the European Security and Defense Identity (ESDI), of key elements of the NATO military command structure and NATO assets, subject to a number of conditions. But the

---

57. Kahler (1995).

United States remains adamantly opposed to any separate European caucus within the NATO Council. American officials fear that such a caucus would render European preferences and decisionmaking opaque rather than transparent and present lowest-common-denominator positions that are inflexible. If such a caucus had been operating during the 1990s, the alliance would very likely have not reached agreement on Bosnia, Kosovo, or NATO enlargement, among other actions. The preformed EU position might well have been either opposed to military action or, in the case of enlargement, unacceptable to the United States.[58]

Paralysis at the international level is sensitive to the decision rule within the EU caucus. Robert Putnam's analogy to two-level games applies here.[59] Putnam's framework applies to bargaining that takes place at both the international and "domestic," in this case, regional, levels. He shows that the larger the set of international agreements that are also ratifiable domestically (the "win set"), the greater the probability of achieving a successful agreement. But countries also have incentives to capture greater shares of joint gains for themselves in distributive bargaining, and countries with a narrow range of ratifiable solutions skew agreements in their favor, because their negotiators' threats to break off bargaining are credible.

Applying this framework to U.S.-European bargaining under the monetary union, the larger the majority required for the Council of Ministers to approve international monetary agreements, the smaller the win set under the euro. A high ratification threshold will reduce the likelihood of U.S.-EU agreement and skew any agreements that are concluded toward European preferences. Unanimity or consensus decisionmaking in the Council is not consistent with an EU that is able to come to a common position in a reasonable period of time that represents something more than a take-it-or-leave-it offer to foreign partners. American policymakers should thus prefer a lower rather than a higher ratification threshold within the monetary union.

58. I am indebted to Ambassador Robert Hunter for a number of points raised in this paragraph.
59. On the development of this metaphor as an analytical framework, see Putnam (1984, 1988). Evans, Jacobson, and Putnam (1993) apply the framework to eleven cases of bargaining over security, economic, and North-South issues.

The unanimity requirement for decisionmaking within the Council on exchange rate regimes should be troubling to U.S. policymakers. On other external matters where a qualified majority is required under the treaty, such as the issuance of "general orientations" regarding exchange rates, the EU's foreign partners must question whether consensus might prevail in practice.[60] Consensus decisionmaking on fiscal policy among the euro-11 will almost surely impede transatlantic fiscal coordination, although that has been conducted only rarely in the past. The more progress that can be achieved toward qualified or simple majority voting on exchange rate and economic policies in Ecofin—the Council meeting in the configuration of economics and finance ministers—the faster will be EU decisionmaking and the more flexible the European bargaining position.

U.S. officials also prefer transparency to opaqueness in decisionmaking within the Council of Ministers. Transparency within the Council, in Ecofin in particular, is remarkably low for such an important body. The meetings are closed to the public; no minutes are released; no voting record is publicized. Although formal conclusions are presented and leaks are pervasive, the European public has no official record of national governments' positions on critical matters within the Council. Hence states are able to shield themselves from societal pressures when instituting reforms, but this comes at the cost of democratic accountability, an issue on which the institutions of the European Union have increasingly come under fire.[61]

Now that Ecofin is empowered with a leading role in external monetary policy, the level of transparency in the Council, in addition to the decision rule, is of considerable interest to the international community. With transparency, American negotiators could identify the preferences of national governments, the dispersion of those preferences, and the flexibility of national positions. They could thus mold U.S. proposals to ensure ratifiability within Europe or to broker bargains

60. The Treaty of Rome specifies that external trade policy also be set by qualified majority voting (QMV), when in fact Community decisionmaking for decades was characterized largely by consensus of at least the large member states under the Luxembourg compromise.

61. On the Council of Ministers as an institution, see, among others, Nugent (1991); Wessels (1991); Peters (1992); Wallace (1996); and Dinan (1999). The *Financial Times*, in particular, has led a crusade for greater transparency within this body.

among the Europeans on matters of American interest. Furthermore, in the language of two-level games, American officials would be able to more accurately assess the "win set" of the monetary union. Doing so is clearly less feasible when the postures of European actors and intra-European differences are opaque.

The United States therefore has a hierarchy of preferences for outcomes regarding EU institutional evolution and the arrangements through which American officials relate to the monetary union (see table 1-1). The first preference is consolidated representation in bilateral bargaining and international institutions, such as the finance G-7, combined with (qualified) majority decisionmaking and transparency. Here, the United States would get the benefits of consolidation—a smaller group, greater confidentiality, and lower transaction costs—while avoiding the lowest-common-denominator syndrome and inflexible EU positions. The second preference is unconsolidated representation under a consensus rule with opaque decisionmaking. This preference is closest to the status quo. The third preference is consolidated representation combined with consensus decisionmaking without transparency. Here the United States is most likely to be confronted with minimalist offers and inflexible positions without being able to discern which governments might be blocking agreement and their true preferences. The question for American policymakers is who to deal with in bilateral, plurilateral, and multilateral forums on monetary and exchange rate matters, national or Community officials? Because consolidated representation of the euro area could leave the United States either better or worse off, depending on the EU's progress in shifting toward majority voting and transparency, American policymakers confront a dilemma.

Fortunately, institutional reform is on the European agenda. First, the Treaty of Amsterdam mandates greater openness in EU institutions, particularly with respect to access to documents and the openness of meetings such as those of the Council. EU institutions are at present implementing this commitment.[62] Second, as a prerequisite to enlargement of EU membership to countries of Central and Eastern Europe, the European Union is committed to convening an intergov-

---

62. European Parliament (1998, 1999).

TABLE 1-1. *Hierarchy of U.S. Preferences Regarding Euro-Area Representation and Decisionmaking*

Preference	External representation	Internal decisionmaking
First	Consolidated	QMV; transparent
Second	Unconsolidated	Consensus; opaque
Third	Consolidated	Consensus; opaque

ernmental conference to consider institutional reform. Member states will review majority voting, voting weights, and the composition of the Commission, among other matters, and propose appropriate amendments to the European treaties. In addition to improving the EU's credibility and appeal as a bargaining partner, member states could streamline and democratize EU decisionmaking through progress on institutional reform. While decisionmaking and transparency fall well short of U.S. preferences, the evolution of EU institutions offers hope for improvements.

It is too early to render a definitive conclusion as to the ultimate impact of the monetary union on the interests of the United States and the rest of the world. That impact depends on several subsequent decisions on the part of the European Union and member states. A positive, mutually beneficial outcome depends, as this discussion has shown, on the provision of stability in Central and Eastern Europe, economic policy reform, and further development of EU institutions and external monetary decisionmaking.

EU External Monetary Policymaking, Representation, and Policy

Granting the Community exclusive competence for internal and external monetary policy greatly affects the external policymaking machinery, the EU's international representation, and the structure and operation of international economic organizations in which European countries are members. Member states attempted to address these matters during the negotiations leading to the Maastricht Treaty but were unable to achieve a consensus. Although they have made recent progress on some items with the arrival of monetary union, the external monetary arrangements of the euro area are evolving slowly.

The Council, European Central Bank, and Maastricht Treaty

Article 109 is the principal section of the Maastricht Treaty that addresses the machinery for making the external policies of the monetary union, including exchange rate policies.[63] Exchange rate policy will be formulated by the regular governing institutions of the European Union—the European Commission, Council of Ministers, and European Parliament—with the important addition of the European Central Bank.[64] The article is reasonably clear with respect to institutions' prerogatives in the conclusion of formal exchange rate agreements. Because it addresses legally binding agreements, however, the treaty has difficulty establishing principles and procedures for informal accords.[65]

Paragraph 1 establishes the procedure for concluding "formal agreements on an exchange-rate system for the [euro] in relation to non-Community currencies." Any resurrection of a fixed-rate system, such as the Bretton Woods regime, or a formal target-zone or global EMS regime that included the dollar and the yen would fall under this procedure. The paragraph gives the Council of Ministers, meaning specifically the Ecofin Council, the ultimate responsibility to conclude formal agreements but not the sole responsibility. As in most other matters of Community competence, the Council would act on a recommendation from the Commission, or the ECB. The Council thus could not act unless the Commission or the ECB took the initiative and submitted a recommendation. Regardless of the source of initiative, the Council must consult the ECB "in an endeavor to reach a consensus consistent with the objective of price stability." In addition, the Coun-

63. See also Articles 3a, 70, 72, 73b-g, 105, and 109 of the Maastricht Treaty; Articles 3, 5.1, 6, 8.3, 12.5, 23, 30, and 31 of the statute of the European System of Central Banks (ESCB); and Declarations 5, 6, 8, and 10 of Council of the European Communities and Commission of the European Communities (1992).

64. The ECB sits at the center of the ESCB, which comprises all fifteen of the national central banks in the European Union. Consistent with common usage, this essay uses these labels when referring to the central banking system of the euro area specifically, although the ECB has invented its own term, "Eurosystem," for the euro-11.

65. For further analysis of the treaty provisions, see Henning (1997).

cil must consult the European Parliament, a simple procedure that does not require parliamentary assent. Critically, the Council must act unanimously in taking the monetary union into a formal regime.

Paragraph 2 states that the Council may "formulate general orientations for exchange rate policy." The Council would act by a qualified majority, rather than unanimity, on a recommendation of the Commission or the ECB. "These general orientations shall be without prejudice to the primary objective of the ESCB [European System of Central Banks] to maintain price stability." The paragraph is remarkably short given that it will bear heavily on relationships with the dollar and the yen. It leaves several critical ambiguities, such as the extent to which orientations are binding on the ECB, who determines whether orientations are prejudicial to price stability, and the relationship between orientations and informal international agreements.[66]

During the drafting of the Maastricht Treaty, the European governments grappled with the questions of what external representation the monetary union should have and how formal exchange rate agreements and broader monetary accords, such as those that might come before the finance G-7 and International Monetary Fund, should be negotiated. The national governments indicated that they did not want the negotiation and conclusion of monetary and exchange rate agreements to follow the procedures used in other international accords, such as those in the trade field. Beyond this, however, they were not at all clear on how the negotiating arrangements for monetary bargaining should differ from those for trade bargaining and were unable to reach a consensus. Paragraphs 3 and 4 therefore instead laid down the procedures by which the negotiating and representational arrangements would be decided later by the Council. The clearest, and perhaps most important, sentence in paragraph 3 stipulates that the arrangements must "ensure that the Community expresses a single position." Also, the Commission must be "fully associated" with the negotiations. Paragraph 5 says simply, "without prejudice to Community competence and Community agreements as regards economic and monetary union, Member States may negotiate in international bodies and conclude international agreements."

66. See also Kenen (1995).

Prudence might have counseled that the European Union take certain steps well before the creation of the euro area: namely, fill in the holes in the external monetary policymaking machinery and operationalize those parts that were addressed by the treaty. Even several months after the event, however, many basic institutional questions remained unresolved. The European Central Bank clearly holds responsibility for foreign exchange operations. Ecofin has reserved for itself a leading role in the formation of external monetary policy. But the line between policy formation and operations is sometimes obscure. The mechanisms by which Ecofin and the ECB would consult internally and with one another, when, for example, contemplating an intervention, have been similarly vague. Moreover, the balance of prerogatives between the two institutions, and with respect to the Commission, is unclear, as are Ecofin's prospects for mustering a sufficient consensus to act on external monetary matters.

Were Ecofin incapable of taking action, authority over this policy domain would flow by default to the ECB. Some central bankers might prefer that outcome, but it would entail substantial risks for the bank, for the euro's external policy, and for international stability. A coherent central bank alone would not be sufficient for a number of international contingencies. Financial relations with countries such as Russia, international financial rescues, and even foreign exchange intervention have a heavy political content and are generally negotiated by political authorities. A central bank whose transparency and democratic accountability were under scrutiny, such as the ECB, would be well advised to secure political cover for external monetary operations.

Representation

Serious discussion of the international representation of the euro area began in mid-1998. On December 1, Ecofin proposed a set of arrangements that were also endorsed by the Vienna European Council meeting of a few days later. The decision applied to representation at three levels—bilateral, finance G-7, and IMF—and was contingent on acceptance by others, specifically the United States, Japan, Canada, and members of the IMF.[67] The arrangements were also characterized as

67. "Finance G-7" refers to the meetings of finance ministers and central bank governors from the Group of Seven countries: the United States, Japan, Germany, France, Britain, Italy, and Canada. It is distinct from the summit meetings of heads of government.

pragmatic and temporary, to be developed further as the monetary union evolved.

Ecofin proposed that a three-member Community delegation attend these international forums, one member being the ECB president. Beginning in October 1998, the ECB president was invited to attend discussions of the world economic outlook, multilateral surveillance, and exchange rate policies in the finance G-7 meetings.[68] The second member, the Council presidency, was chosen to represent the political authorities. When a non-euro country holds the presidency, the chair of the euro-11 council would attend. Hence a new seat would have to be created at the finance G-7 table when Germany, France, or Italy does not hold the presidency. The third member of the delegation was to be a representative of the Commission, "in the capacity of providing assistance to the president of Ecofin/Euro-11."[69]

The euro-area position in these meetings was to be prepared first by the Economic and Financial Committee (EFC), the successor to the Monetary Committee, then informally by the euro-11 council, and then formally by Ecofin as a whole. On matters going beyond the competence of the Community (that is, reserved for member states) and beyond the particular interests of the euro-11 countries (such as fiscal policy), the ministers suggested that they might "formulate and present common understandings" that would serve as the basis for positions taken in the finance G-7 and other groups. The ministers cited the examples of Russia and the international financial system as issues on which such common understandings might be needed.[70]

Introducing the monetary union itself as a member of the IMF would probably require an amendment to the Fund's Articles of Agreement. Rather than pursue this radical change, Ecofin again sought a pragmatic solution, suggesting that the views of the Community be represented in the Executive Board by the executive director of the member state serving as the chair of the euro-11 council. (Note, however, that several

68. For a broader discussion of the ECB's role in external representation of the euro area, see Tommaso Padoa-Schioppa, "The External Representation of the Euro Area," statement to the European Parliament, Subcommittee on Monetary Affairs, Brussels (March 17, 1999).
69. Ecofin (1998).
70. Ecofin (1998).

euro-area countries do not have elected executive directors in the board.) This executive director would be assisted by a representative from the Commission.[71] Separately from this proposal, the Executive Board has granted observer status in its meetings to the ECB.

The ministers came to no fixed configuration for bilateral representation to third countries, saying that such arrangements would vary with circumstances, and that "it is the responsibility of the presidency of the Council/Euro-11 to make the necessary arrangements." Thus, despite significant progress, the European Union had not answered the question, to paraphrase Henry Kissinger's famous quip, whom should the Secretary of the Treasury telephone when trying to coordinate a concerted intervention or organize a financial rescue?

The United States and other non-European members of the G-7 rejected the December 1998 Ecofin proposal for that forum. After intensive negotiations, in which the German presidency and U.S. Treasury took the leading roles, a compromise was agreed at the G-7 meeting in Frankfurt in June 1999, which established the representational arrangements on a provisional basis. These arrangements are described in greater detail in the section below on institutional adaptation.

Exchange Rate Policy

What exchange rate policy might the monetary union decide to pursue in relation to the dollar, yen, and other non-European currencies? Provisions of the Maastricht Treaty strongly favor a policy of flexibility, which is also favored by the relative closure of the euro area and the absence of clearly defined institutional machinery for an activist policy of exchange rate stabilization. Official statements at the outset of the monetary union and policy during its first six months suggested that the euro area would be inclined to adopt a laissez-faire posture toward the external value of the euro, treating it as the residual of domestic macroeconomic policy.

The European Council considered the exchange rate policy for the euro and the mechanisms through which that policy would be established when meeting in Luxembourg on December 12 and 13, 1997. The presidency conclusions contained the following paragraph:

71. Ecofin (1998).

The Council should monitor the development of the exchange rate of the euro in the light of a wide range of economic data. . . . *While in general exchange rates should be seen as the outcome of all other economic policies,* the Council may, in *exceptional* circumstances, for example in the case of a clear misalignment, formulate general orientations for exchange rate policy in relation to non-EC currencies in accordance with Article 109 (2) of the Treaty. These general orientations should always respect the independence of the ESCB and be consistent with the primary objective of the ESCB to maintain price stability. (Emphasis added)

Meeting together with central bank governors in a subsequent informal Ecofin retreat, the finance ministers reaffirmed that general orientations would be issued rarely. Central bank officials consistently expressed skepticism regarding currency stabilization in relation to the dollar.

During the creation and first months of the monetary union, European policymakers expressed contradictory positions on exchange rate policy. In late 1998 and early 1999, some officials suggested a disposition toward less flexible exchange rates. At the press conference after the victory of Germany's Social Democratic Party (SPD) and Green Party, Chancellor-elect Gerhard Schröder and Finance Minister–designate Oskar Lafontaine announced that target zones for exchange rates would be a top priority of their government. The new German government later moderated this objective to the institution of "constrained flexibility" among the major currencies. Lafontaine then resigned his post abruptly in March 1999. France's finance minister Dominique Strauss-Kahn, who had urged German officials to moderate their activist position, proposed a "system of enhanced cooperation" on macroeconomic policies that would bring greater stability to currencies and perhaps lay the foundation for a G-7 consensus on limiting exchange rate fluctuation.[72]

In December 1998 Wim Duisenberg, president of the ECB, commented that the exchange rate for the euro "is one of the main indica-

---

72. Peter Norman, "France proposes forex stability plan," *Financial Times,* February 9, 1999, p. 2. See also *Financial Times,* February 17, 1999.

tors that we watch. But I am more fearful of volatility than the level. We have to avoid that to the maximum extent possible." He continued: "As things stand, I don't exclude the euro being a strong currency. We don't want the exchange rate to unduly undermine the competitiveness of 'Euroland' with the rest of the world." An appreciation of the euro would constitute a tightening of monetary conditions, he suggested, and would give the ESCB greater room to reduce interest rates. The central bank, he added, would watch the exchange rate closely and not follow a policy of benign neglect.[73]

These comments appear to have been designed to reassure the markets that, while adhering to a hands-off posture toward the exchange rate, European authorities would not neglect the external value of the new currency. Fundamentally, the ECB and ESCB have been opposed to currency stabilization or even activist exchange rate policy on the grounds that it could distract domestic monetary policy from the primary purpose of securing internal price stability. Independent central bankers in general and European central bankers in particular harbor an abiding suspicion that governments could use exchange rate policy to extract a monetary policy more to their liking. Other statements of Duisenberg are more reflective of this basic position: "Just as a fever cannot be prevented by restricting the movement of the thermometer, we cannot ensure the absence of exchange rate pressures simply by announcing targets for exchange rates. The pursuit of stability-oriented monetary and fiscal policies at home constitutes a fundamental prerequisite for fostering a stable exchange rate environment."[74]

At the inception of the monetary union, the exchange rate stood at $1.17 to the euro. In the first half of 1999, the euro steadily *declined* in value, nearing parity to the dollar. During this decline, European officials made numerous contradictory statements about the importance and desirability of the slide. Too many European officials were talking about the exchange rate. As of this writing, moreover, European authorities have engaged in no foreign exchange intervention to support their currency.

73. Wolfgang Muenchau, Peter Norman, and Lionel Barber, "Duisenberg says ECB would not welcome overvalued euro," and "Builder of the euro team spirit," *Financial Times*, December 7, 1998, pp. 3 and 23.

74. *Eurecom*, February 1999, p. 3.

The emphasis on the fiscal-monetary policy mix could be construed as indirect activism with respect to the exchange rate. The national central banks, coordinating through the European Central Bank in early December 1998, reduced interest rates in the expectation that fiscal policy would remain tight within the euro area in 1999. The bargain is implicit, rather than explicit, and is vulnerable to changing circumstances. If in the face of rising unemployment governments were to abandon fiscal restraint, the bargain could well be off, and a new policy mix could replace the present "Clinton-Greenspan" mix.[75] Under those circumstances, the monetary union would no longer be pursuing a competitive exchange rate via the policy mix.

It is still too early to make definitive conclusions about the exchange rate policy that will be pursued by the euro area. The tension between those favoring a managed exchange rate policy and those favoring a more flexible currency regime has yet to play itself out. Although the emphasis on the policy mix might constitute attention to the exchange rate indirectly, the experience of the first half-year of the monetary union with respect to currencies directly is broadly consistent with predictions of benign neglect.

Summary

The European Union has not yet clearly defined the institutional mechanisms to support even modest activism in external monetary policy. The mechanisms by which exchange rate policy will be formulated are as yet incomplete and untested. At the international level, the finance G-7 agreement in Frankfurt on the external representation of the euro area represents progress. However, the viability of these arrangements remains to be seen. Further development of policymaking institutions at the European level would be necessary for the EU presidency or chair of the euro-11 council to articulate a common external monetary policy and negotiate on these matters with the G-7 partners. If the EU fails to develop these institutions and policy processes, the Council might well effectively cede its preroga-

---

75. See, for example, James Blitz, "Budget target relaxation 'wrong'," *Financial Times,* May 28, 1999, p. 3. See also Tony Barber, "Put to the test by conflicting needs," *Financial Times,* May 28, 1999, survey 7.

tives in the external monetary arena to the ECB, in which case the euro area would lack coherent political authority to serve as the counterpart to the U.S. Treasury in addressing an important range of international monetary and financial contingencies that contain a political dimension.

Adaptation of International Institutions

The redesign of international institutions in light of monetary union, whether at the bilateral, plurilateral, or multilateral level, confronts two pervasive tensions within the structure of the European Union. One is the tension between the centralization of monetary and exchange rate policy and the relative decentralization of fiscal, financial, and general economic policy. This tension could bifurcate the two broad issue areas and complicate issue linkages. At the international level, however, governments and central banks of the large industrial countries have generally not made such linkages adroitly and have done so with decreasing frequency. The opportunity cost to bifurcating international coordination in this way is thus correspondingly small.

Second, tension exists between the prerogatives of national governments and those of the monetary union (or Community) in international institutions.[76] For political reasons, national governments are fighting tooth and nail to maintain their direct representation in these forums, citing provisions in the Maastricht Treaty and international protocols to support their position. Over the short to medium term, they will thus have their cake (monetary union) and eat it (retain national representation) too.

Over the long term, however, several forces are likely to press for the replacement of national governments by Community institutions. First, provisions of EU law will over time press member states to accept the full consequences for representation that arise from the Maas-

76. Consistent with formal EU terminology, the word "Community" is sometimes used here interchangeably with the monetary union. The monetary union is a project of the whole Community, notwithstanding the fact that at the outset four member states were either in derogation of their commitment to the single currency or held an exemption from that commitment. As a legal concept, the term "Community" also survives the changeover to the name "European Union" with the Maastricht Treaty.

tricht Treaty obligation to pursue a common external monetary policy and articulate that policy with unity. Second, representation by the monetary union will be more efficient for international bargaining and political transactions. Third, as experience in dealing with the monetary union accumulates, the international community itself could well press for more streamlined representation as well.

Finance G-7

Recently, meetings of the finance G-7 have been held three or four times a year. Most, though not all, of these meetings include the central bank governors. The gatherings are prepared by the deputy finance ministers and, especially when the governors will be attending, often central bank officials. Each meeting usually begins with a presentation by the managing director of the IMF on the economic outlook followed by a multilateral surveillance discussion of the member economies. After the IMF officials leave the room, the ministers and governors discuss exchange rate policies and measures. The discussion then turns to the subject of the day, which has recently been the financial crises and redesign of the "international financial architecture." The deputies' meetings have become important in their own right as a mechanism of subcabinet-level cooperation. Although the president of the European Commission and the presidency of the EU Council of Ministers attend the annual summit meetings, the Commissioner for Economic and Financial Affairs attends only those portions of the finance G-7 devoted to certain specialized topics, such as Russia. Before 1999, the EU presidency did not attend at all.

How should this forum be adapted to the presence of the monetary union over the long run? Analysts have offered a number of proposals. C. Fred Bergsten and Randall Henning recommend that the finance G-7 be transformed into a G-3.[77] Henning recommends that monetary and exchange rate matters be handled in a "monetary G-3" while the broader financial and economic matters be discussed, perhaps in back-to-back meetings, in the full G-7, subject of course to the European Union settling on a satisfactory decision rule and external representation.[78]

77. Bergsten and Henning (1996).
78. Henning (1997).

David K. Begg, Francesco Giavazzi, and Charles Wyplosz object that the latter proposal would bifurcate discussions of monetary and fiscal policies, which are interdependent. Hence the monetary union must be represented in these discussions directly, rather than through one of the member states, and this will require increasing, not reducing, the number of participants. Although this new configuration will be "messy," it is considered "inevitable."[79]

Barry Eichengreen and Fabio Ghironi emphasize the asymmetry between fiscal decentralization and monetary centralization within the European Union, also predicting greater rather than less complexity in the finance G-7.[80] In this view, it is unlikely that the finance G-7 will be converted into a G-3, and the scope for strengthening transatlantic monetary cooperation will be more limited after the formation of the euro area.

As already discussed, U.S. interests in the consolidation of the G-7 are mixed. Having all of the present G-7 players at the table is arguably in the interest of the United States.[81] Rather than being presented with the one, common position by, for example, the EU presidency and the ECB president, the United States would hear as well from the German, French, and Italian finance ministers and central bank governors. U.S. officials would be able to sense for themselves the preferences of national governments and the flexibility of their positions and formulate proposals accordingly. Securing agreements would be less feasible when U.S. authorities have a restricted view of the dispersion of preferences among European officials.

Three problems arise, however, with this otherwise compelling consideration. First, keeping an "American seat at the European table" is complicated by distributional bargaining. Aware that U.S. officials could use information about national preferences to extract a greater share of joint gains from international bargains, the Europeans might well want to exclude intra-European bargaining from the G-7, arriving at the meeting with a common position but in just as many numbers. Second, the European members of the G-7 do not comprise all of the

---

79. Begg, Giavazzi, and Wyplosz (1997). Kenen (1998) concurs.
80. Eichengreen and Ghironi (1998).
81. McNamara (1998).

relevant actors at the European level. Without the EU presidency, the smaller countries would be completely excluded. Their preferences and views are critical, given the fact that "general orientations" on exchange rate policy will be determined in the Council of Ministers by a qualified majority, requiring 44 votes among the 65 votes of the members of the euro area. In matters beyond the monetary area, a qualified majority is 62 out of a total of 87 votes. The combined votes of France, Germany, and Italy are only 30; including Britain raises this to 40, still short of a winning majority. So, the European members of the G-7 will still have to bargain with their small and midsized brethren. The United States will not be able to cut a deal with only the large European governments. Third, American authorities are averse to discussing sensitive exchange rate matters, for example, with many people around the table. Managing such sensitive discussions in a broad forum could be risky and perhaps impracticable.

In the manner that these institutions are actually evolving, full consolidation of the G-7 into a G-3 is not a near-term prospect. When the Vienna Council meeting of December 1998 proposed the tripartite delegation from the Community *in addition to* the national finance ministers and central bank governors, Americans objected. Their concerns extended beyond the number of Europeans around the table to the institutions of the Commission and the presidency.

American officials discounted the role of the Commission in the external matters of the monetary union. If the Commission were needed to initiate a Council decision on general orientations, for example, it could be brought into a meeting on an ad hoc basis, they reasoned. Despite the December 1998 Vienna agreement, some national finance ministries were also less than enthusiastic about including the Commission and conveyed this lack of enthusiasm to their American counterparts. The politics of external representation on each side of the Atlantic thus became very much entwined.

U.S. officials resisted the inclusion of the presidency in the finance G-7 for primarily two reasons: stature and continuity. Dealing with small-state presidencies was not particularly useful or necessary, they contended originally, and the six-month rotation of the presidency creates a lack of continuity. With eleven members of the monetary union, one cycle takes five and a half years, and that period will lengthen as membership in the euro area increases. Most small-country finance ministers will thus attend no more than two G-7 meetings before disappearing and never being seen again in that particular forum.

The smaller member states were nonetheless adamant regarding representation by the chair of the euro-11 council in these meetings and pressed the case. After six months of negotiations, the finance G-7 agreed that its meetings would be split into two parts, each with a different configuration. The first part, which would focus on the world economic outlook, multilateral surveillance, and exchange rates, would be attended by the ECB president and the chair of the euro-11 council, along with the seven finance ministers and the central bank governors of the United States, Japan, the United Kingdom, and Canada.[82] The national central bank governors of the euro-area member states would be excluded until the second part of the meeting, devoted to the broader set of issues relating to the international financial system, which would not necessarily include the ECB president and euro-11 chair. The Commission would be invited to take part on specific issues, such as assistance for Russia, which has been on the agendas of most such meetings. These arrangements would apply for an indefinite period of time.[83]

The June 1999 agreement represents significant progress. Nonetheless, several important questions remain unanswered about how the euro area will participate under this configuration. First, limited primarily to the question of which officials go to international meetings, the Ecofin decisions say virtually nothing about what these officials should say about substantive policy matters when they arrive. Second, although the ECB, EFC, euro-11 council, and full Ecofin will in all likelihood prepare those substantive positions, how these institutions will work together in formulating policy remains unclear. Third, it is unclear what latitude the Community delegation would have to respond to proposals from the Americans, Japanese, Canadians, and British at these meetings. Finally, the arrangements for ratifying any

---

82. This configuration was anticipated by Alogoskoufis and Portes (1991, p. 233).

83. Robert Chote, "Europe bank chiefs reduce G7 presence," *Financial Times*, June 15, 1999, p. 5.

agreement reached in these meetings are vague, to say the least. It would be wholly unacceptable for the euro-11 chair to simply read a prepared statement to the G-7 in the name of the euro area and be unable to negotiate accords for joint action.

International Monetary Fund

The International Monetary Fund will be a particularly important arena of cooperation and competition between the United States and the European Union. Since the creation of the IMF more than a half century ago, Europeans have been conscious and sometimes resentful of American influence within the institution, headquartered in Washington, D.C. A number of European officials see EMU as an opportunity to counter American influence with collective influence of their own. At stake, among other matters, are the restoration of international financial stability and the construction of a new international financial "architecture" that could reduce the frequency and severity of financial crises.

An outstanding case of American arm-twisting in the IMF was the February 1995 loan to Mexico in the wake of the peso crisis. The amount of the loan, $17.8 billion, was unprecedented for the IMF and seven times the size of Mexico's quota, the usual basis for determining the amount that a member country may draw. The U.S. Treasury persuaded the Fund staff to back the request and then persuaded the membership to approve the loan in the Executive Board. But the executive directors from Britain, Germany, the Netherlands, Belgium, Switzerland, and Norway, four of whom lead constituencies encompassing more than thirty other countries, registered their protest by abstaining from the loan approval. Whether the monetary union will change the outcome of similar decisions in the future is a critical question for U.S. interests, the IMF, and international financial cooperation in general.

The monetary union poses a number of other IMF-related questions: How will monetary union alter the patterns of influence within the IMF? Will the United States contend with an equally powerful partner within the institution? What will be the respective roles of the monetary union and its member states? To what degree will the union itself have a voice within the Fund versus relying on officials from

47

member states to speak for the euro area? Could the monetary union itself ever become a member of the IMF? How will the IMF adapt its multilateral surveillance procedures?[84]

To play a role equal to that of the United States, the members of the euro area would have to combine their influence within the IMF. Collectively, the euro-11 hold more than 22 percent of the quotas of the IMF, substantially more than the U.S. share, which is 18.3 percent. (The EU15 hold roughly 30 percent of total quotas.) Because voting power is proportionate to quotas, the member states of the monetary union could in principle carry greater weight within the IMF and wield a collective veto over important decisions.

EU member states are tenaciously committed to maintaining separate representation at the Fund, however, citing in their defense Article 109, paragraph 5, and the Fund's Articles of Agreement stipulating that only countries are members. But as members of the monetary union, the member states are also committed to pursuing a common external monetary policy. Over what range of issues within the IMF are European governments required to adhere to a common position? This question has not been explicitly addressed and answered by the member states.

Matters that materially affect the external monetary position of the euro area should clearly fall within this scope. Any decision on the exchange rate for the euro and the flexibility or rigidity of the exchange rate regime would certainly be a matter of common policy, requiring a unified euro-area position. But would this apply to a decision to increase IMF quotas? A decision to create a new lending facility? A lending decision that affects the reserve position of the euro members? A distribution of Special Drawing Rights (SDRs)? A Fund decision to borrow from another organization or member government? The admission of new members? The expulsion of recalcitrant members? A decision regarding IMF staff, such as the selection of the managing director?

In prior years, whenever it was concerned that the Fund was straying from its original mission, the German government was fond of re-

84. See, for example, Polak (1997); Thygesen (1997); Henning (1997); Eichengreen and Ghironi (1998); McNamara (1998).

minding its partners that the institution was principally an International *Monetary* Fund. Similarly, Wim Duisenberg and André Szàsz have stated that "primary functions of the IMF are clearly monetary."[85] Such statements would seem to convey a presumption that Fund matters would fall under the obligation to pursue common (external) monetary policies. In practice, however, European governments do not appear to have conceded that any IMF issue falls within the obligation to pursue a common external monetary policy. Instead, they argue that IMF matters should be the subject of "common understandings" among the euro-11 and other EU members that should provide the basis for coordinating the positions which European executive directors take in the IMF Executive Board. This reasoning rests on the premise that while speaking with multiple voices at cross-purposes in the Executive Board would reduce European effectiveness in the IMF, it would not violate any legal obligation under the EU treaties.

At the outset of the monetary union, the IMF extended to the European Central Bank the right to send a representative to Executive Board meetings. The ECB representative attends meetings on the world economic outlook, multilateral surveillance of the euro area and individual countries within the monetary union, and the role of the euro in the international monetary system, among other topics, and has the right to speak at such meetings. The representative is not automatically invited to other meetings of the Executive Board, such as surveillance discussions of non-European countries and discussions about the international financial architecture.[86] Ecofin proposed that the EU presidency or chair of the euro-11 council represent the monetary union in the Fund through its executive director, which would require European-level coordination but not Executive Board approval. Ecofin also proposed that when presenting the views of the Community, the executive director be assisted by a representative from the Commission. For the moment, however, the Executive Board appears unlikely to permit Commission officials to attend its meetings.

The structure of representation of members of the IMF within the

---

85. See Duisenberg and Szász (1991), quoted in Louis (1997).
86. IMF (1998).

Executive Board, the "constituency system," brings formidable centrifugal pressure to bear on any common position of the governments of the euro area. The eleven members of the monetary union sit in eight constituencies. Belgium, Austria, and Luxembourg share a constituency with seven other countries. The Netherlands leads a constituency of nine non-EU European countries plus Israel. Spain sits in a constituency dominated by Latin America. Ireland sits in a constituency composed of Caribbean countries plus Canada and represented by a Canadian executive director. Presenting a coordinated EU position while balancing constituency interests will be a difficult act indeed.

These minimal arrangements for representing the monetary union at the IMF and giving expression to the common external monetary policy are a temporary compromise with the bureaucratic prerogatives of member-state finance ministries and central banks. They almost certainly do not constitute a "stable institutional equilibrium." Some issues will probably arise that will prove too divisive for mere coordination by executive directors. When a difference arises on the exchange rate for the euro, the financial stability of an important neighbor, perhaps even an applicant for EU membership, or a matter that materially affects the external reserve position of the euro area, any failure to adhere to a common position could well be justifiable. Member states and the Commission would have an incentive, and indeed might well be obliged, to bring such a case before the Court of Justice.

Even if not feasible in the short term, could the European presence in the IMF be consolidated over the long term? Several possible developments could clear the path for consolidation. First, with the creation of the monetary union secured, and if Britain decided to join the euro area, those within the Community advocating for the center could well pay less deference to the bureaucratic prerogatives of national finance ministries and central banks. Second, successfully grappling with institutional reform in anticipation of enlargement of the EU membership to Central and Eastern Europe—reforms deferred in the Treaty of Amsterdam—could also facilitate consolidation. Further movement toward majority voting would be a prerequisite, from the perspective of the international community, for consolidated representation of the euro area in international institutions. Third, further international financial crises or shocks, on which euro area members have contrasting interests yet require quick decisionmaking, could demonstrate the weakness of representative arrangements wherein national governments have their cake and eat it too. In this hypothetical, but not implausible, environment, one could envision amending the IMF's Articles of Agreement to provide for membership on the part of the European Union.[87]

Conclusions and Recommendations

Monetary union is likely to be in the American geopolitical interest, because it is likely to buttress economic and political stability in Central and Eastern Europe. European strength within the region will probably serve U.S. interests because the United States and European Union share core political values of rule of law, democracy, and human rights and the United States is eager to economize on resources devoted to foreign contingencies. The impact on American economic interests is somewhat more complex. If growth within the monetary union were stifled by inflexibility at the microeconomic level and the euro area relied on exports as a principal source of growth, U.S.-EU monetary relations could well resemble U.S.-German relations during the 1960s and 1970s, which witnessed repeated conflicts over macroeconomic and exchange rate policies. On the other hand, the monetary union itself could well enhance prospects for structural reform, raising investment and growth. Moreover, even if the euro were to tighten potential balance of payments constraints on the United States, this could have a silver lining in preventing the United States from making policy mistakes, such as the overexpansionary monetary policies in the 1970s and fiscal policies in the 1980s. In short, though monetary union is likely to be in the interest of the United States overall, it could also present some obstacles and inconvenience in the more narrow international monetary area.

If, over the coming decade, the European Union did not play a constructive role in Central and Eastern Europe, structural reforms were frozen, or institutional reforms failed, this favorable conclusion about

87. Henning (1997, pp. 50–57, 65–67).

the benefits of the monetary union outside of Europe would have to be reassessed. Similarly, if basic monetary preferences of the United States and euro area diverged—they are reasonably convergent at the moment—the potential for conflict would increase.

The European Union and euro-11 are in the midst of a long-term evolution of the institutional arrangements for making external monetary policy and presenting that policy to the international community. Competence for policy—as distinct from operational matters—is reasonably clear and centralized within the European System of Central Banks. Many questions on the political side of external monetary policymaking remain open, however: whether governments of the member states will agree on actions, the specific mechanisms by which such agreements could be reached, how common positions will be represented to international organizations and third countries, and how international agreements would be discussed and ratified.

At the international level, the finance G-7 agreement in Frankfurt on the external representation of the euro area represents progress. However, the effectiveness of these arrangements should be monitored. Further development of policymaking institutions at the European level will be necessary for the EU presidency or chair of the euro-11 council to articulate a common external monetary policy and negotiate on these matters with partners in the finance G-7 and IMF. Without such mechanisms, the U.S. Treasury would have no coherent counterpart within the euro area when addressing politically sensitive international monetary and financial questions. The interests of the rest of the world are closely connected in particular to the decision rule and transparency of the policymaking process within the euro area.

In this era of flexible exchange rates when priority is given to domestic macroeconomic conditions, one might ask whether it is necessary to have a well-functioning system of international monetary and financial cooperation. The sentiment behind this question appeals to those analysts who favor a completely hands-off posture toward the foreign exchange market and international financial crises. However, even ad hoc financial rescues or foreign currency intervention will be difficult to execute without G-7, bilateral, and internal policymaking mechanisms in place. The recent Asian and global crises provide ample proof of the need for collective action in the financial area. The present pattern of growth and payments balances supplies evidence of the need for a similar capacity in the monetary area.

Two specific causes for concern are the unprecedented U.S. trade deficit in 1999 and the shakiness of the coalition supporting openness in international economic policy, the latter demonstrated by two failed votes on fast-track trade negotiating authority in the 105th Congress. Although the buoyant domestic economy and the low rate of unemployment have contained the backlash to "globalization" in the United States, those favorable domestic conditions will certainly change at some point. If the mid-1980s serves as any guide, macroeconomic and exchange rate cooperation might well be desirable under those new circumstances. Only the most extreme laissez-faire proponents can afford to be complacent about the health of international monetary and financial cooperation. Those who favor at least ad hoc cooperation, not to mention more ambitious schemes, should be quite concerned about euro-area policymaking and the adaptation of international institutions. At least three courses of action could be taken to help redress these institutional deficiencies and improve transatlantic and international monetary cooperation in the presence of the euro. They have to do with the U.S. stance on representation, EU external policymaking, and official competition over currencies.

U.S. Stance on Representation

The United States should clearly enunciate a long-run vision for the institutional arrangements by which it wishes to work with the monetary union in bilateral, plurilateral, and multilateral forums in the future. That statement should articulate the principles that guide U.S. policy and specify American preferences for provisional and permanent solutions. As pointed out earlier, streamlining the euro area's external monetary policymaking and consolidating its representation would have substantial benefits in terms of efficiency and bargaining costs. However, such centralization would be inferior to the status quo from the standpoint of the interests of the United States and other countries outside of Europe if the Community operated by consensus without transparency. The United States need not wait until the member states are ready to cede their authorities to the Community in external monetary relations before asserting these basic interests.

53

Specifically, U.S. authorities should urge the European Union to move substantially further toward qualified majority voting and transparency in decisionmaking. If the coming intergovernmental conference makes substantial progress on the decision rule and transparency, and if the United Kingdom joins the monetary union, the way will then be paved for working with the euro area through the Community institutions and for consolidating external representation. Such a consolidation could transcend the removal of national central bank governors of the euro area during the first part of finance G-7 meetings, as decided at the June 1999 Frankfurt meeting, and could eliminate the finance ministers themselves eventually. Under these circumstances, forming the "monetary G-3" and holding back-to-back meetings with the finance G-7 would be possible.

Given the uncertainty regarding the decision rule, lack of transparency, and the continuing contention within the EU over institutional matters, the United States should of course work within the provisional Frankfurt arrangements. American policymakers should use these arrangements as an opportunity to interact with the EU presidency (and the chair of the euro-11 council), urging the Council to prepare the presidency well and to streamline policymaking and bargaining arrangements in general. Once the political integration of the European Union has developed substantially further, the obligations of member states to adhere to a common external monetary policy and speak with one voice in international forums might well be more fully enforced. The United States would then have fewer choices in the entities it can deal with directly in Europe, and it would benefit from having nurtured authority and respect for the Community institutions and efficient policymaking within the monetary union.

The streamlining of external monetary policy and consolidation of representation of the EU also have ramifications for the balance of influence *within* the United States, between the Department of the Treasury and the Federal Reserve. To the extent that the European Union creates a full partner for the U.S. Treasury in the form of a Council that is able to act, the present balance between the Treasury and Fed on external monetary policy can be preserved. If the Council cedes authority over external monetary policy to the ECB by default, the balance would probably shift toward the Fed. International recognition of the Council, EU presidency, and euro-11 chair, as well as the Commission, in light of their responsibilities under the Maastricht Treaty and subsequent decisions, would reinforce the political pole for external monetary policy within the euro area.

EU External Policymaking

The European Union has more work to do on the institutional setup for external monetary policymaking and negotiations. Although Ecofin and the European Council have made progress recently, the mandate of the presidency to negotiate with the United States, Japan, Britain, and Canada in the finance G-7 remains unclear. At the bilateral level, it remains to be seen how Ecofin and the ECB will in practice work through the presidency and president, respectively, to intervene in foreign exchange markets and mount financial rescues, for example, in concert with the United States. Ecofin should continue to address these matters.

Ecofin should first confirm publicly that the presidency or euro-11 chair will be its external monetary representative in plurilateral and bilateral relations, as the Frankfurt G-7 decision would suggest. *Assuming that is the case, the European Union should give the presidency a mandate to negotiate agreements, both formal and informal, within the G-7 and with other political authorities as circumstances (such as a major financial crisis) require and should agree in advance to procedures for quickly ratifying (or rejecting) any agreement that the presidency, in consultation with the ECB and the Commission, negotiates.* These provisions appear to be necessary to avoid the pattern that has developed in transatlantic trade negotiations, which would be particularly damaging in the monetary arena, where quick, decisive, and sometimes stealthy action by policymakers is required from time to time.

Where possible, the Council should avoid consensus decisionmaking and move further toward qualified majority voting on external monetary matters. The Council should also fulfill transparency obligations under the Treaty of Amsterdam, which would of course apply to Ecofin in particular. The European Council meeting in Cologne in June 1999 decided to convene the next intergovernmental conference in early 2000 to consider institutional reform. The extension of qualified majority voting is on that agenda and should be pursued. Transparency should be added to the agenda and pursued as well.

Official Competition over Currencies

The United States and the European Union should foreswear official competition over the international use of their currencies. The international monetary environment may be unstable over the next several years: exchange rate volatility could increase and portfolio rebalancing will occur. Current account imbalances are rising and international financial instability remains a threat. A multiple reserve currency system has enough instability built into it without the additional factor of official conflict over the international roles of the dollar and the euro. A rapid shift from one equilibrium to another, promoted by European measures to boost the euro, could have disruptive consequences for the global economy and bring Europe into open confrontation with the United States. "Predatory policy initiatives," as Benjamin J. Cohen writes, "could provoke retaliatory countermeasures with each side endeavoring to defend or promote the competitiveness of its own money."[88] Competitive interest rate increases, or refusal to lower interest rates when easing would otherwise be justified, would be a particularly damaging and senseless form of U.S.-EU rivalry.

As far as the private international roles for the dollar and euro are concerned, investors, debt managers, importers, exporters, currency traders, and other private actors should, through the sum total of their separate choices, determine the "market shares" of these currencies. The choices of these actors should not be constrained by government policy. Currencies should play roles concomitant with their merits, as determined by the size and characteristics of the national economies that stand behind them. The role of the euro, in particular, should reflect the size, breadth, liquidity, and diversity of the European capital market. I expect the euro to displace, not replace, the dollar substan-

---

88. Cohen (1998, p. 160) advocates U.S.-EU cooperation to ensure the smooth introduction of the euro into the international monetary system: "The Euro's entry onto the world stage must be explicitly managed." I advocate that national governments and the European Union adopt a neutral stance with respect to currency roles in private markets. But, with respect to the official roles of the these currencies, in foreign exchange holdings, for example, I concur with Cohen.

tially in many roles over time. But that displacement should follow from progress in regional financial integration rather than be induced artificially through official programs.

Inducements to adopt the euro as a vehicle currency, issuance of large denomination notes to capture underground seigniorage, and government contracting that manipulates the denomination of invoices would not be constructive. The liberalization of national capital markets and removal of barriers to investment and financial services within the European Union, on the other hand, would create growth, employment, and wealth. Financial liberalization and integration would be a legitimate and unobjectionable form of competition with the United States. Europeans who are intent on capturing a larger share for the euro would be well advised to focus their competitive energies on creating a regional financial market that rivals that of the United States. In so doing, they would not only avoid the dangers of direct currency competition but also increase European growth prospects. The United States and the rest of the world should welcome this form of competition, because the efficiency and growth benefits to them would outweigh the losses associated with reduced roles for non-European currencies.

References

Alogoskoufis, George, and Richard Portes. 1991. "International Costs and Benefits of EMU." *European Economy,* special edition (1): 231–45.

_____. 1992. "European Monetary Union and International Currencies in a Tripolar World." In *Establishing a Central Bank: Issues in Europe and Lessons from the US,* edited by Matthew Canzoneri, Vittorio Grilli, and Paul R. Masson, 273–300. Cambridge University Press.

_____. 1997. "The Euro, the Dollar and the International Monetary System." In *EMU and the International Monetary System,* edited by Paul R. Masson, Thomas H. Krueger, and Bart G. Turtelboom, 58–78. Washington, D.C.: International Monetary Fund.

Andrews, David M. 1998. "The U.S. and Europe's Single Currency." Working Paper 1998/9. Copenhagen: Danish Institute of International Affairs.

Andrews, David M., and Thomas D. Willett. 1997. "Financial Interdependence and the State: International Monetary Relations at Century's End." *International Organization* 51 (Summer): 479–511.

Bank for International Settlements. 1996. *International Banking and Financial Market Developments.* Basel, Switzerland (May).

Begg, David K., Francesco Giavazzi, and Charles Wyplosz. 1997. "Options for the Future Exchange Rate Policy of the EMU." Occasional Paper 17. London: Centre for Economic Policy Research.

Bénassy, Agnes, A. Italianer, and Jean Pisani-Ferry. 1994. "The External Implications of the Single Currency." *Economie et Statistique.* Special issue on *Economic and Monetary Union*, 9–22. Paris: Institute for Statistics and Economic Studies.

Bénassy, Agnes, Benoît Mojon, and Jean Pisani-Ferry. 1997. "The Euro and Exchange Rate Stability." Paper prepared for the IMF–Camille Gutt Conference on EMU and the International Monetary System, Washington, D.C. (March 17–18).

Bénassy-Quéré, Agnes. 1996. *Potentialities and Opportunities of the EURO as an International Currency.* Economic Papers 115. Brussels: European Commission, Directorate-General for Economic and Financial Affairs.

Bergsten, C. Fred. 1997a. "The Impact of the Euro on Exchange Rates and International Policy Cooperation." In *EMU and the International Monetary System*, edited by Paul R. Masson, Thomas H. Krueger, and Bart G. Turtelboom, 17–48. Washington, D.C.: International Monetary Fund.

_____. 1997b. "The Dollar and the Euro." *Foreign Affairs* 76 (July/August): 83–95.

Bergsten, C. Fred, and C. Randall Henning. 1996. *Global Economic Leadership and the Group of Seven.* Washington, D.C.: Institute for International Economics.

Cameron, David R. 1996. "Moving to Economic and Monetary Union: Transitional Issues, Third-Stage Dilemmas." Yale University. Photocopy (Fall).

_____. 1997. "Economic and Monetary Union: Underlying Imperatives and Third-Stage Dilemmas." *Journal of European Public Policy* 4 (September).

Centre for European Policy Studies (CEPS). 1998. *Capital Markets and EMU.* Report of a CEPS Working Party. Brussels.

Cohen, Benjamin J. 1994. "Beyond EMU: The Problem of Sustainability." In *The Political Economy of European Monetary Unification*, edited by Barry Eichengreen and Jeffry Frieden, 149–65. Boulder, Colo.: Westview Press.

_____. 1997. "L'Euro contre le Dollar: Un Defi pour Qui?" *Politique Etrangère* 4.

_____. 1998. *The Geography of Money.* Cornell University Press.

Cooper, Richard N. 1992. "Will an EC Currency Harm Outsiders?" *Orbis* 36 (Fall): 517–31.

_____. 1999. "Key Currencies after the Euro." *World Economy* 22 (January): 1–24.

Corden, Max. 1972. *Monetary Integration.* Essays in International Finance 93. Princeton University, International Finance Section.

Council of the European Communities and Commission of the European Communities. 1992. *Treaty on European Union.* Brussels-Luxembourg: Office of Official Publications of the European Community.

Destler, I. M., and C. Randall Henning. 1989. *Dollar Politics: Exchange Rate Policymaking in the United States.* Washington, D.C.: Institute for International Economics.

De Grauwe, Paul. 1997. *The Economics of Monetary Integration.* 3d ed. Oxford University Press.

Dinan, Desmond. 1999. *Ever Closer Union?* 2d ed. Boulder, Colo.: Lynne Reinner.

Dobson, Wendy. 1991. *Economic Policy Coordination: Requiem or Prologue?* Policy Analyses in International Economics 30. Washington, D.C.: Institute for International Economics.

Dornbusch, Rudi. 1996. "Euro Fantasies." *Foreign Affairs* 75 (September/October): 110–25.

Duisenberg, W. F., and A. Szàsz. 1991. "The Monetary Character of the IMF." In *International Financial Policy: Essays in Honor of Jacques J. Polak,* edited by Jacob A. Frenkel and Morris Goldstein, 254–66. Washington, D.C.: International Monetary Fund.

Ecofin Council. 1998. "Report to the European Council on the State of Preparation for Stage 3 of EMU, in Particular the External Representation of the Community. Brussels (December 1).

Edison, Hali J., and Linda S. Kole. 1994. *European Monetary Union Arrangements: Implications for the Dollar, Exchange Rate Variability and Credibility.* International Finance Discussion Paper 468. Washington, D.C.: Board of Governors of the Federal Reserve System.

Eichengreen, Barry. 1996. "How to Avoid a Maastricht Catastrophe." *International Economy* (May/June): 16–20.

Eichengreen, Barry and Jeffrey A. Frankel. 1996. "The Future of the SDR." In *The SDR, Reserve Currencies, and the Future of the International Monetary System,* edited by Michael Mussa and others, 337–78. Washington, D.C.: International Monetary Fund.

Eichengreen, Barry, and Jeffry Frieden. 1994. "The Political Economy of European Monetary Unification: An Analytical Introduction." In *The Political Economy of European Monetary Unification,* edited by Barry Eichengreen and Jeffry Frieden. Boulder, Colo.: Westview Press.

Eichengreen, Barry, and Fabio Ghironi. 1998. "European Unification and International Monetary Cooperation." In *Transatlantic Economic Relations in the Post–Cold War Era,* edited by Barry Eichengreen, 69–98. New York: Council on Foreign Relations.

Emerson, Michael. 1999. "Cosmos, Chaos and Backbone for a Wider European Order." Working Document 130. Brussels: Centre for European Policy Studies.

Emerson, Michael, and others. 1999. "A System for Post-War South-East Europe." Working Document 131. Brussels: Centre for European Policy Studies.

European Central Bank (ECB). 1999. "The International Role of the Euro." *Monthly Bulletin* (August).

European Commission. 1990. "One Market, One Money." *European Economy* 44 (October).

————. 1997. "External Aspects of Economic and Monetary Union." Staff Working Document. Brussels: European Commission.

European Commission, Directorate-Generale for Economic and Financial Affairs. 1995. *Report on the International Economic Order.* Brussels: European Commission.

European Council. 1996. "Presidency Conclusions." Meeting Communiqué. Dublin.

European Parliament, Committee on Institutional Affairs. 1998. "Report on Openness within the European Union." Session document A4-0476/98. Brussels: European Parliament (December 8).

_____. 1999. "Resolution on Openness within the European Union." Brussels (January 12).

Evans, Peter B., Harold K. Jacobson, and Robert D. Putnam, eds. 1993. *Double-Edged Diplomacy: International Bargaining and Domestic Politics.* University of California Press.

Feldstein, Martin. 1997a. "EMU and International Conflict." *Foreign Affairs* 76 (November/December): 60–73.

_____. 1997b. "The Political Economy of the European Economic and Monetary Union: Political Sources of an Economic Liability." *Journal of Economic Perspectives* (Fall).

_____. 1992. "The Case against EMU." *Economist,* June 13, 12–19.

Frankel, Jeffrey A. 1995. "Still the Lingua Franca: The Exaggerated Death of the Dollar." *Foreign Affairs* 74 (July/August): 9–16.

_____. 1998. Comments to a Conference on EMU and International Monetary Stability Sponsored by the Luxembourg Institute for European and International Studies, Luxembourg (December 3–4).

Frankel, Jeffrey A., and Andrew K. Rose. 1998. "The Endogeneity of the Optimum Currency Area Criteria." *Economic Journal* 108 (July): 1009–25.

Fratianni, Michele, Andreas Hauskrecht, and Aurelio Maccario. 1999. "Dominant Currencies and the Future of the Euro." In *Ideas for the Future of the International Monetary System,* edited by Michele Fratianni, Dominick Salvatore, and Paolo Savona, 97–121. The Netherlands: Kluwer.

Frenkel, Jacob A., and Morris Goldstein. 1999. "The International Role of the Deutsche Mark." In *Fifty Years of the Deutsche Mark: Central Bank and the Currency in Germany since 1948,* edited by Deutsche Bundesbank, 685–730. Oxford University Press.

Geithner, Timothy F. 1998. "The EMU, the United States, and the World Economy." Speech to a conference of the Konrad-Adenauer-Stiftung and Aspen Institute Berlin, Washington, D.C. (May 7).

Gros, Daniel. 1996a. *Towards Economic and Monetary Union: Problems and Prospects.* CEPS Working Paper 65. Brussels: Center for European Policy Studies.

_____. 1996b. "A Reconsideration of the Optimum Currency Area Approach: The Role of External Shocks and Labour Mobility." *National Institute Economic Review* 158 (April): 108–18.

Gros, Daniel, and Niels Thygesen. 1992. *European Monetary Integration: From the European Monetary System to European Monetary Union.* New York: Longman.

Hall, Peter A., and Robert J. Franzese Jr. 1998. "Mixed Signals: Central Bank Independence, Coordinated Wage Bargaining, and European Monetary Union." *International Organization* 52 (Summer): 505–36.

Hartmann, Philipp. 1996. *The Future of the Euro as an International Currency: A*

Transactions Perspective. CEPS Research Report 20. Brussels: Centre for European Policy Studies.

Henning, C. Randall. 1994. *Currencies and Politics in the United States, Germany, and Japan.* Washington, D.C.: Institute for International Economics.

————. 1996. "Europe's Monetary Union and the United States." *Foreign Policy* 102 (Spring): 83–100.

————. 1997. *Cooperating with Europe's Monetary Union.* Policy Analyses in International Economics 49. Washington, D.C.: Institute for International Economics.

————. 1998. "Systemic Conflict and Regional Monetary Integration: The Case of Europe." *International Organization* 52 (Summer 1998): 537–73.

————. 1999. *The Exchange Stabilization Fund: Slush Money or War Chest?* Policy Analyses in International Economics 57. Washington, D.C.: Institute for International Economics (April).

Ilzkovitz, Fabienne. 1996. *Prospects for the Internationalization of the EURO.* Doc. II/362/96-EN, European Commission, Directorate-General II Economic and Financial Affairs. (June).

International Monetary Fund (IMF). 1997. *International Capital Markets.* Washington D.C.

————. 1998. "IMF Grants Observer Status to European Central Bank." Press Release 98–64. Washington, D.C.

Iversen, Torben. 1998. "Wage Bargaining, Central Bank Independence, and the Real Effects of Money." *International Organization* 52 (Summer): 469–504.

Johnson, Karen. 1994. "International Dimension of European Monetary Union: Implications for the Dollar." International Finance Discussion Paper 469. Washington, D.C.: Board of Governors of the Federal Reserve System.

Kahler, Miles. 1995. *Regional Futures and Transatlantic Economic Relations.* New York: Council on Foreign Relations Press.

Kenen, Peter B. 1969. "The Theory of Optimum Currency Areas: An Eclectic View." In *Monetary Problems of the International Economy,* edited by Robert Mundell and Alexander Swoboda. University of Chicago Press.

————. 1995. *Economic and Monetary Union: Moving Beyond Maastricht.* Cambridge University Press.

————. 1998. "EMU and Transatlantic Economic Relations." HWWA Discussion Paper 60. Hamburg, Germany.

Livingston, Robert Gerald. 1998. "The Euro and Peace." Letter to the editor. *Foreign Affairs* 77 (March/April): 181.

Louis, Jean-Victor. 1997. "Comments on Polak and Thygesen." In *EMU and the International Monetary System,* edited by Paul R. Masson, Thomas H. Krueger, and Bart G. Turtelboom, 534–39. Washington, D.C.: International Monetary Fund.

McKinnon, Ronald. 1963. "Optimum Currency Areas." *American Economic Review* 53: 717–25.

McNamara, Kathleen R. 1998. "European Monetary Union and International Economic Cooperation." Report on a workshop organized by the International Finance Section, Princeton University (April 3).

Masson, Paul R., and Bart G. Turtelboom. 1997. "Characteristics of the Euro, the Demand for Reserves, and Policy Coordination under EMU." In *EMU and the International Monetary System*, edited by Paul R. Masson, Thomas H. Krueger, and Bart G. Turtelboom, 194–224. Washington, D.C.: International Monetary Fund.

Meyer, Laurence H. 1999. "The Euro in the International Financial System." Speech to a conference of the European Institute, Washington, D.C. (April 26).

Mundell, Robert. 1961. "A Theory of Optimal Currency Areas." *American Economic Review* 51: 657–65.

Nugent, Neill. 1991. *The Government and Politics of the European Community.* 2d ed. Duke University Press.

Peters, B. Guy. 1992. "Bureaucratic Politics and the Institutions of the European Community." In *Euro-Politics: Institutions and Policymaking in the "New" European Community*, edited by Alberta M. Sbragia, 75–122. Brookings.

Pisani-Ferry, Jean. 1996. "Variable Geometry in Europe: Implications for External Relations." Centre des Etudes Prospectives et d'Informations Internationales. Photocopy (June).

Polak, Jacques J. 1997. "The IMF and Its EMU Members." In *EMU and the International Monetary System*, edited by Paul R. Masson, Thomas H. Krueger, and Bart G. Turtelboom, 491–511. Washington, D.C.: International Monetary Fund.

Porter, Richard D., and Ruth A. Judson. 1996. "The Location of U.S. Currency: How Much Is Abroad?" *Federal Reserve Bulletin*, October, 883–903.

Portes, Richard, and Hélène Rey. 1998. "The Emergence of the Euro as an International Currency." *Economic Policy* 26 (April): 305–32.

Program on International Policy Attitudes. 1998. *Seeking a New Balance: A Study of American and European Public Attitudes on Transatlantic Issues.* Washington, D.C.: Center for the Study of Policy Attitudes and the Center for International and Security Studies at Maryland.

Putnam, Robert D. 1984. "The Western Economic Summits: A Political Interpretation." In *Western Summits and Europe: Rivalry, Cooperation, and Partnership*, edited by Cesare Merlini, 43–89. London: Croom Helm.

———. 1988. "Diplomacy and Domestic Politics: The Logic of Two-Level Games." *International Organization* 42 (Summer): 427–60.

Putnam, Robert D., and C. Randall Henning. 1989. "The Bonn Summit of 1978: A Case Study in Coordination." In *Can Nations Agree? Issues in International Economic Cooperation*, by Richard N. Cooper, Barry Eichengreen, C. Randall Henning, Gerald Holtham, and Robert D. Putnam, 12–140. Brookings.

Rey, Hélène. 1997. *International Trade and Currency Exchange.* CEPR Discussion Paper 322. London: Centre for Economic Policy Research (February).

Rogoff, Kenneth. 1998. "Blessing or Curse? Foreign and Underground Demand for Euro Notes." *Economic Policy* 26 (April): 263–303.

Thygesen, Niels. 1997. "Relations among the IMF, the ECB, and the IMF's EMU Members." In *EMU and the International Monetary System*, edited by Paul R. Masson, Thomas H. Krueger, and Bart G. Turtelboom, 512–30. Washington, D.C.: International Monetary Fund.

Thygesen, Niels, and ECU Institute, eds. 1995. *International Currency Competi-*

tion and the Future Role of the Single European Currency. London: Kluwer Law.

U.S. Senate, Committee on the Budget. 1997. *Europe's Monetary Union and Its Potential Impact on the United States Economy.* 105 Cong. 1 sess. Washington, D.C.: GPO.

Wallace, Helen. 1996. "The Institutions of the EU: Experience and Experiments." In *Policymaking in the European Union,* edited by Helen Wallace and William Wallace, 37–70. Oxford University Press.

Wessels, Wolfgang. 1991. "The EC Council: The Community's Decisionmaking Center." In *The New European Community: Decisionmaking and Institutional Change,* edited by Robert O. Keohane and Stanley Hoffmann. Boulder, Colo.: Westview Press.

2

The Role of the Euro

in the International System:

A European View

Pier Carlo Padoan

WITH THE INTRODUCTION of the euro in early 1999, debate began almost immediately on its potential as a global currency. That debate is essentially about how the euro-dollar exchange rate will evolve over the next five to ten years, during the initial phase of European Economic and Monetary Union (EMU). It presupposes that the international financial system before EMU consisted of multiple currency regions in equilibria and that the system is now in transition between a regional, or "low," equilibrium to a global, or "high," equilibrium. As made clear in chapter 1, the course of events during this transition will greatly depend on the policymaking machinery and options chosen by EMU authorities, most notably the exchange rate policy. This chapter explores those options and their possible effect: on European growth; on the economies of Central and Eastern Europe, the Mediterranean, and Latin America; and on transatlantic cooperation.

Multiple Equilibria and the Transition Phase

In the aftermath of EMU, some analysts have argued that the euro is bound to be weak in relation to the dollar initially.[1] For one thing, they

1. For perhaps the strongest criticism of the euro project, see Feldstein (1997).

say, markets will be unable to identify with sufficient accuracy the monetary policy strategy of the European Central Bank (ECB), especially if it looks as though the new institution's independence may be challenged. For another, the euro area will include economies that do not offer all the guarantees for respecting the criteria of a strict fiscal policy. Furthermore, the highly heterogeneous economies belonging to EMU will, at least in the medium term, pressure the ECB to accommodate their monetary policies, in view of asymmetrical shocks that might hit individual countries or regions within EMU. Hence the ECB will have to struggle to build its own reputation in the field, especially if the markets prefer to stick to dollar-denominated investments.

Other observers have a different view of the euro's prospects, for they think that structural factors will generate an excess demand for the new currency (and a resulting excess supply of dollars).[2] Such factors are likely to include shifts in the composition of private portfolios and changes in the demand for euros and dollars as official reserve currencies.[3] A more sophisticated argument in support of appreciation, based on the portfolio approach to exchange rate determination, is that the euro will undergo an initial revaluation that will overshoot the long-term equilibrium value; and this will push up the euro interest rate, incorporating devaluation expectations that would occur to compensate the initial appreciation.[4] Others suggest that the elimination of a large number of national currencies in the European Union (EU) will increase the volatility of the euro-dollar rate, leading to higher interest rates owing to the greater risk associated with such volatility.[5]

The initial weakness of the euro in relation to the dollar is understandable in view of the growth differential between the United States and "Euroland."[6] Much of the reason for this difference lies in "structural" rather than in "macroeconomic" imbalances in the EU economy, although the behavior of the euro-dollar rate will also be greatly influenced by economic policy. At least four major structural and insti-

2. See, for example, Bergsten (1997); Alogoskoufis and Portes (1997).
3. Bergsten (1997) estimates that portfolio diversification (and thus excess demand for the euro) will range from $500 billion to $1,000 billion dollars, while excess dollar reserves will range from $50 billion to $200 billion.
4. See Alogoskoufis and Portes (1997).
5. See Bénassy, Benoît, and Pisani-Ferry (1997).
6. Some of the weakness of the euro can be ascribed to the Kosovo crisis.

tutional changes are likely to occur: the elimination of a substantial portion of international trade (which becomes regional trade within EMU), the disappearance of a number of national currencies and of their respective markets, the introduction of a completely new currency, and the creation of an important new central institution (the ECB). The first three changes, which are structural, will interact with the ECB's policy, and the external value of the euro rate will reflect this (complex) interaction. All in all, the international monetary system is on the brink of enormous changes.

The possible course of the euro's evolution can be assessed both through the standard theory of exchange rate determination and through the theory of "key currencies," as the euro is a natural candidate for the role of international currency alongside the dollar. Several conditions must be met for a currency to take up this key role: the economy that supports the currency must have significant weight in world trade and product, there must be no significant external constraints, capital must enjoy full freedom of movement, financial markets should be deep and liquid, and the economy must be strong and stable.[7] The euro (and EMU) satisfies—or will soon be able to satisfy—these requisites.

In the first instance, Europe is already ahead of the United States with a 31 percent share of world trade (excluding infra-EU trade) and 20 percent of world product, versus 26 percent and 18 percent, respectively, for the United States. External constraints, which may be defined as the economy's need to draw resources from the rest of the world, also seem negligible: in the past two decades, the European Union has maintained a substantially balanced current account— which has recently turned into a surplus—whereas the United States has shown a deficit (figures 2-1, 2-2). Capital movement poses no problems, either. The euro's composition and, to some extent, the U.K. government's decision not to participate in the first phase of EMU do, however, leave the financial market in euros less developed than that of the United States. As for European strength and stability, much will depend on the extent to which the European Union succeeds in restoring sustainable growth and employment. For these reasons, the euro

7. See, for example, Bergsten (1996).

FIGURE 2-1. *EU Sectoral Financial Balances, 1980–95*

Percentage of GDP

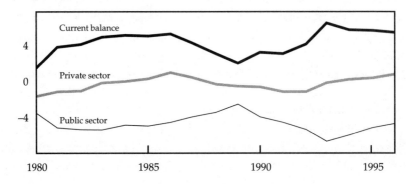

FIGURE 2-2. *U.S. Sectoral Financial Balances, 1980–95*

Percentage of GDP

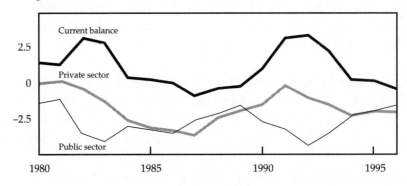

can be reasonably expected—at least in the medium term—to be the second key currency alongside the dollar. What remains to be seen is whether the euro will be more or less equivalent to the American currency or whether it will merely remain a "regional" currency.

In theory, multiple equilibria can occur in the evolution of key currencies owing to the presence of externalities associated with the role of "vehicle currency."[8] The equilibrium share of a currency in international reserves and private portfolios may be "small" or "large," de-

8. See, for example, Krugman (1992, pp. 75–91); Portes and Rey (1998).

pending on whether it plays a regional or a global role. To shift from one equilibrium to the other, a currency must surpass a minimum critical mass in international use that will allow agglomeration factors, network externalities, to operate.

The concept of multiple equilibria implies a different share for the euro as an international currency and ultimately a different long-term equilibrium level of the euro dollar rate, to the extent that the demand for euros ensuing from its role as a key currency is related to different supply behaviors. Whether the euro will shift from one equilibrium to another will depend largely on EMU policies and on whether the markets and monetary authorities of third countries can be persuaded of the euro's stability as an international currency. If EMU policy focuses on stability, the international demand for euros would probably grow, and there might be a (temporary) revaluation. Conversely, EMU economic policies not conducive to stability would make the European currency less desirable and thus reduce its international role in the long run.

The euro's desirability would, moreover, be enhanced by the perception that once the euro was introduced the EU economy would grow out of its low-growth/high-unemployment profile (see the fifth requisite for a key currency). Hence EU polices in support of growth would have a positive impact on the euro's role in international markets, just as the behavior of the American economy underpins the dollar's attractiveness. An "attractive" euro, in turn, would make the EU economy attractive to international capital. In fact, policies enhancing EU growth would be advantageous for both the European Union and the United States because, among other things, a solid and expanding economic environment tends to strengthen international cooperation. By contrast, periods of low growth tend to breed more conflicts in both monetary and commercial relations.[9]

Economic Policy Options and the Composition of EMU

If multiple equilibria are possible, then the management of economic and monetary policy during the transition is crucial not only for steer-

9. See Padoan (1995).

ing convergence toward a new equilibrium but also for determining the nature of the equilibrium. The question is, what would be a desirable policy for the external value of the euro? Some see two possible answers to this question: an exchange rate policy that promotes internal price stability (through a "strong euro") and one that supports competitiveness (through a "weak euro"). These alternatives refer by and large to nonissues. The most appropriate policy is obviously one that takes the greatest advantage of the characteristics of a common currency. This point may be clarified by drawing on the literature on monetary unions to assess the costs and benefits that EMU members can expect from a common currency.[10]

The benefits of a monetary union increase with the extension of the union, as expressed in terms of either the number of participating countries or of economic size. This relation arises from the fact that the larger the union, the greater the benefits accruing to each member from the elimination of transaction costs and exchange rate uncertainty, besides those stemming from lower variability of interest rates.[11] Furthermore, these advantages increase with the degree of openness of the economies of the union's members. In the European case, it can be deduced that EMU's benefits grow with an increase in the number of member countries, EMU's gross domestic product (GDP), and the degree of integration and openness of the internal market.

Costs, on the other hand, will increase with the diversity of the monetary stabilization policies preferred by the area's policymakers. In other words, the costs of union membership for a country with a high preference for containing inflation will increase if other union members have a strong preference for policies oriented toward income stabilization. In general, the higher the convergence of the member countries' preference for low inflation and stability-oriented monetary policy, the lower the costs. EMU composition could therefore be a crucial issue, except that convergence toward the Maastricht parameters suggests that policy divergences within EMU have already been all but eliminated. Even the least disciplined among the union's

10. The approach used here is based on Collignon (1997).
11. The costs and benefits of monetary unions are amply discussed in the literature. For an overall evaluation, see, for example, De Grauwe (1992).

FIGURE 2-3. *Costs and Benefits of a Monetary Union*

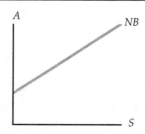

members have enacted rigorous anti-inflationary and fiscal reform policies. Hence the costs of EMU will be quite moderate.

The costs can be said to rise in proportion to the propensity of the Union's members to use monetary policy for income stabilization, as depicted by A in figure 2-3. Increasing values of A fuel inflation in the union and hence diminish monetary stability. Because of the economies of scale introduced by a common currency, benefits will rise as the size of S, the extension of the union, grows. Line NB is the locus of the points where benefits and costs offset each other (net benefits equal zero). NB is an increasing function because more monetary activism may be offset by an expansion of the union's size. The slope of NB reflects the degree of openness of the Union's member economies. The points above NB indicate net negative benefits: there is no incentive to create a monetary union. The opposite occurs below the line. Increasing propensity toward monetary activism for a given size of the union clearly results in net negative benefits and must be offset by enlarging the union or by encouraging greater openness (increasing the slope of NB) in order to raise the scale benefits.

This approach can now be applied to a currency region, defined as an extension of the area of currency use, which therefore includes countries that are not members of the union.[12] The size of the currency region is clearly greater than that of the currency union only in the case of key currencies such as the dollar, the deutsche mark, and the euro.

A currency region differs from a currency area in that the latter encompasses countries that agree formally to a fixed exchange rate or to

12. See Cohen (1998).

FIGURE 2-4. *Costs and Benefits of a Currency Region*

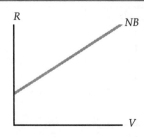

a monetary union, whereas the former covers the geographic area in which a given currency is used without reference to that currency's legal status. In other words, the size of a currency region depends on the behavior of markets and not on formal agreements. Such a region is therefore measured by the extent to which a vehicle currency is used for international transactions, which in turn depends largely on the utilization of network externalities that go with such a role.[13]

In this case (see figure 2-4), the costs R of the use of the key currency by domestic and foreign agents (and thus not only public bodies but also, and mainly, private operators) rise with the growing use of the exchange rate to support the union's exports. This behavior can be described as an "activist" use of the exchange rate because it not only depresses the value of the currency but also increases the currency's instability, by weakening its role both as a store of value and as a vehicle currency. Thanks to benefit externalities, the benefits V rise as the currency's use in international markets rises. In this case, too, the points of zero net benefits are located along NB, and points above (below) the schedule indicate net negative (positive) benefits. As figure 2-4 also shows, markets continue to use a given currency as vehicle even if its exchange rate tends to become unstable, if the use of the currency is so extensive that it offset the costs of instability, owing to network externalities. The dollar is an obvious case in point.

It can therefore be concluded that the external benefits of EMU will increase as the size of the euro's currency region increases, in other words, as the euro becomes more widely used by countries and oper-

13. See Krugman (1992, pp. 75–91); Portes and Rey (1998).

ators outside EMU. The costs associated with the euro's external dimension—that is, of using the euro as an international currency—will increase as more EMU member countries decide to pursue "activist" exchange rate policies for the euro in relation to third-country currencies (primarily the dollar) in order to promote exports via real devaluation. In this case, too, net (external) benefits of the currency will depend on EMU's composition. I will return to this point later, for it suggests that the net benefits of EMU would be maximized by a stable external value of the euro.

If an international reserve currency can have multiple equilibria in the international monetary system, and if the euro should locate itself in a low-equilibrium value, then external monetary policy for the euro should endeavor to reach a high equilibrium; that is, it should attempt to broaden the size of its currency region from that covered by the deutsche mark to one that is proportional to the economic size of the European Union. The prospects of the European currency region can thus be assessed by examining, first, the features of and options for the exchange rate policy of the euro and, second, the potential for the extension of its currency region.

EMU as an Endogenous Currency Area: Some Preliminary Evidence

The greatest reservations about the sustainability of a monetary union in Europe can be found in the literature on optimal currency areas. The leading argument there is that the changeover to a single currency will deliver net benefits only if the countries involved are not subject to asymmetric shocks.[14] Otherwise, the optimum choice is independent monetary policies that can offset the lack of synchronism of business cycles and absorb specific shocks occurring in different economies. To illustrate, the area gravitating about Germany has, in the past, experienced asymmetrical shocks in relation to those that have affected the rest of the European economy.[15] Others argue that a stylized split exists between core and peripheral Europe, as indicated

14. This paragraph draws on Centro Europa Ricerche (CER) (1998, chap. 2).
15. See Bayoumi and Eichengreen (1992).

by the volatility of real exchange rates and the different degrees of synchronization of the trade cycles.[16] Such a split suggests that a limited currency union is possible, but that the currency will become more unstable as it is adopted by a greater number of countries.

The theory of optimal currency areas raises some questions, however, regarding its methodology and the practical relevance of the issues it addresses. Trade integration and the synchronization of business cycles, for instance, are likely to increase with increasing monetary integration, so the foregoing objections would be met ex post by the countries that will join EMU.[17] This point is important to keep in mind, especially if one accepts the idea that the single currency will require a wholesale redefinition of the economic policy model pursued by the European countries.[18] Furthermore, the possible asymmetrical shocks to exports—which bear most of the cost from loss of the exchange rate—would in any case have limited impact on growth and employment creation in the single European countries.[19] In addition, cyclical correlations ought to be analyzed in two directions rather than merely with reference to the ties between the different European countries and the system's center economy. Further hints of the possible endogeneity of EMU as a currency area can be found in the evidence on macroeconomic and regional convergence.

Convergence of Economic Cycles

A monetary union can be sustained if its national economic cycles converge. Where cyclical patterns differ, the sensitivity to exogenous shocks also differs, and the consequences of such shocks will be asymmetrical.[20] The concept of an endogenous currency area appears to go hand in hand with such convergence, in that monetary integration deepens trade integration and leads cyclical profiles to converge.[21]

To illustrate, figure 2-5 compares correlation coefficients among the

16. See Artis and Zhang (1995).
17. As emphasized by Frankel and Rose (1996).
18. See Allsopp and Vines (1996); Fantacone (1997).
19. See Gros (1996).
20. Bayoumi and Eichengreen (1992).
21. Some evidence of this can be found in Frankel and Rose (1996).

FIGURE 2-5. *Cyclical Correlation in the European Union, 1972–92*

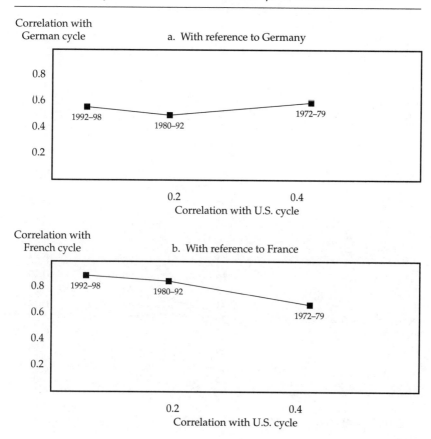

GDP cycles of "Euroland's" largest countries with those of Germany and the United States over three periods.[22] Because the evolution of the German cycle is distorted by the process of unification, the correlation with the French cycle is also presented. Points shown on the curves indicate a marked diversification over time with respect to the U.S. cycle. In the case of the French cycle, the curve shifts upward, indicating a higher coefficient of correlation with the other European economies. This is not present in the German case because of the consequences of unification. As table 2-1 shows, increasing cyclical corre-

22. For a similar analysis, see Artis and Zhang (1995).

TABLE 2-1. *Euroland's Cyclical Correlation in Demand Components:*
Correlation with Germany, 1972–98

Demand component	1972–79	1980–92	1992–98
Consumption			
Austria	–0.08	0.57	0.83
Belgium	0.14	0.70	0.72
France	0.72	0.28	0.68
Italy	0.34	–0.32	0.62
Netherlands	0.66	0.57	0.62
Portugal	–0.84	0.65	0.93
Spain	–0.60	0.52	0.76
Average	0.05	0.42	0.74
Dispersion[a]	12.31	0.84	0.15
Investment			
Austria	0.54	0.73	0.62
Belgium	–0.16	0.54	0.75
France	0.52	0.57	0.77
Italy	0.31	0.62	0.34
Netherlands	0.29	0.21	0.00
Portugal	n.a.	n.a.	n.a.
Spain	–0.40	0.53	0.59
Average	0.18	0.53	0.51
Dispersion[a]	2.08	0.33	0.57
Exports			
Austria	0.49	0.57	0.85
Belgium	0.74	0.55	0.65
France	0.65	0.49	0.89
Italy	–0.19	0.76	0.00
Netherlands	0.63	0.57	0.93
Portugal	0.18	0.41	0.84
Spain	0.22	–0.30	0.71
Average	0.39	0.44	0.70
Dispersion[a]	0.86	0.78	0.46

SOURCE: Elaborations on Organization for Economic Cooperation and Development,
Economic Outlook, Statistical Appendix, December 1998.
n.a. Not available.
a. Coefficient of variation.

lation is present in all output components, particularly consumption and exports.

These data confirm that deepening monetary integration is causing a European economic cycle to emerge. The three periods considered relate to different economic policy regimes in Europe: an initial period of flexible exchange rates following the collapse of Bretton Woods (1972–79), the European Monetary System (EMS, 1980–92), and the final period (1992-98), which was marked by the substantial depreciation of several currencies and by an acceleration of convergence toward the single currency.

The relevant point, however, is that convergence took the form of a move toward declining, not expanding, growth rates. The growth of European GDP steadily declined over the period: average growth rates were 3.3 in 1972–79, 2.4 in 1980–92, and 1.6 in 1992–98. This suggests that the countries with initially higher growth rates gradually adapted to the German economy's slower rate: while the French and Italian GDP grew at 3.3 and 3.7 percent, respectively, in the 1970s as against 2.9 percent in Germany, the German economy expanded faster in 1980–92, when the Italian economy was growing more slowly.

A disaggregation of output components also shows a gradual slowing of the growth rates of consumption and investment, although this is less evident for exports. Two factors are notable in this regard. In the first place, German exports rose faster than those of France and Italy in the 1980s; this is especially evident from the West German trend (which does not include the statistical effect of reunification). In the second place, exports are the only accelerating component during the 1990s, which indicates greater dependence of the European economic cycle on foreign trade. Because about two-thirds of the EU's international trade consists of intra-EU trade, this effect is clearly the result of the integration that took place in Europe and is in line with the analysis based on the concept of an endogenous currency area.

Given increasing trade integration in a currency area, one must also take into account the sensitivity of growth to exchange rate movements and the elasticity of employment with respect to growth. The sensitivity of growth to exchange rate changes is one of the factors commonly used to assess the costs and benefits of a single currency, the assumption being that EMU countries differ in their preferences for exchange rate management and that this could create co-ordination problems in the management of the common monetary policy. To the extent that the growth model of the "Mediterranean" members of EMU is somewhat more dependent on the exchange rate, by giving up the exchange rate these countries would be suffering higher costs in terms of growth and employment. In other words, currency unification would be biased by a structural difference in policy preferences.[23]

Evidence of aggregate export functions (see table 2-2) sheds some light on this issue. Consider an initial, quite general, specification where exports of five European countries (Germany, France, Italy, Spain, and the United Kingdom) are expressed as a function of the real exchange rates and of a uniform variable for world demand.[24] Estimation results show that the elasticity of exports to intra-European exchange rates is highest in Germany and lowest in Italy. This implies that, contrary to common belief, the German economy will benefit from the creation of the single currency because it interrupts the real long-term appreciation of the deutsche mark. At the same time, the cost to Italy of giving up intra-European exchange variability is limited because the elasticity of its exports is small (less than 0.5 percent). Germany, next to Spain, also displays the highest export elasticity to the real extra-EU exchange rate. An appreciation of the euro would depress German exports more than those of France and Italy. On the other hand, Italy displays the highest export demand elasticity, in relation to both the European aggregate and the rest of the world. A demand shock would thus affect Italy to a proportionally greater extent.

Estimation results also indicate that the incentive for using the exchange rate as a tool for supporting export activities could be greater in the center country than in countries at the periphery. The greater exchange rate elasticity of German exports may reflect the lower variability of the deutsche mark, whereas the fluctuations of other currencies have often been used merely for smoothing over the cumulative inflation differentials. Nevertheless, the evidence pre-

23. This, of course, makes it more difficult to satisfy Collignon's (1997) criterion.
24. By assuming an identical demand variable for all countries, it is possible to focus the comparison on exchange rate elasticity.

TABLE 2-2. *Estimate of Export Functions in Selected Countries: First Specification, 1975–96[a]*

Logarithms of index numbers

Function	Germany	France	Italy	Spain	United Kingdom
Constant	4.98	3.28	2.65	3.82	0.53
	(9.90)	(3.94)	(5.24)	(2.89)	(1.51)[b]
Real exchange rate	−1.19	−0.72	−0.56	−0.79	−0.10
	(−9.94)	(−3.94)	(−5.17)	(−2.79)	(−1.44)[b]
OECD imports	0.76	0.80	0.87	1.16	0.68
	(38.98)	(38.45)	(47.46)	(24.88)	(36.37)
d_{90}	0.11				
	(4.26)				
Summary statistic					
Adjusted R^2	0.99	0.98	0.99	0.97	0.99
Standard error of regression	0.025	0.031	0.029	0.073	0.025
Durbin-Watson statistic	2.00	0.64	0.87	0.42	0.80
F statistic	604.70	762.92	1,186.70	331.18	888.90

SOURCE: OECD for exports and imports; Banca d'Italia for real exchange rates.
a. Figures in parentheses are t statistics.
b. The coefficient is not statistically different from zero.

sented does not indicate a potential weakening of the euro owing to the greater exchange rate sensitivity of the Mediterranean economies.

As for the effects on employment, these remain in doubt. When Granger tests are used to check for the presence of statistical links between exports, employment, and productivity (table 2-3), the null hypothesis of noncausality is rejected for Germany insofar as relations between exports, on the one hand, and employment and gross fixed capital formation, on the other, are concerned.[25] In turn, there seems to be a Granger causality between gross fixed capital formation and productivity, and between the latter and exports. However, noncausality is rejected even for the relation between productivity and gross fixed capital formation, so the former variable apparently follows a pattern not entirely attributable to exports.

25. These tests were also carried out in Gros (1996).

TABLE 2-3. *Exports and Economic Growth in Selected Countries: Granger Causality Tests*[a]

Variable	Germany	France	Italy	Spain	United Kingdom
Exports > employment	11.3*	0.7	1.5	4.2**	1.7
Exports > gross fixed capital formation	7.9*	0.5	2.7***	0.1	1.5
Exports > productivity	0.0	1.6	0.7	0.8	2.0
Gross fixed capital formation > exports	0.6	0.1	1.6	1.6	0.1
Productivity > exports	8.6*	0.3	0.2	0.8	3.5**
Gross fixed capital formation > productivity	3.0***	0.2	4.7	2.6	1.3
Productivity > gross fixed capital formation	8.4*	1.2	6.3*	1.4	4.6**

a. Asterisks indicate cases for which the null hypothesis of noncausality is rejected at (*) 1 percent, (**) 5 percent, and (***) 10 percent probability.

The results of causality tests are not as clear for other countries. Again, some evidence of a causal relation between exports and growth can be found for Italy, through gross fixed capital formation, while there might be a relation between exports and employment for Spain. When the Granger tests were repeated for extra-EU exports, no significant result was obtained, which is not surprising in view of the low degree of openness of the European economy when intra-area trade is excluded.

Evidence above suggests that the loss of the exchange instrument would not seriously affect long-term growth in most of the European countries because they show little evidence of export-led growth and of exchange rate sensitivity of exports. Although these results support the idea of a sustainable and self-reinforcing EMU, other findings suggest that convergence toward the German cycle has not favored investments and employment.[26] Deceleration on investment in Europe—which can be seen, to some extent, as the cost of monetary and cyclical convergence—has been accompanied by an increase in the labor-saving (capital-deepening) share of capital accumulation over

26. Further evidence of this effect can be found in CER (1999).

total capital formation. This trend suggests that one cost of (getting to) monetary union might be forgone employment opportunities.

Regional Catching Up

The hypothesis that monetary convergence has a positive effect on regional catching up in Europe can be tested using a standard model.[27] A measure of the rate of convergence in a neoclassical model of exogenous growth is obtained by log-linearizing the law of capital-stock movement around the steady state; in the case of a Cobb-Douglas production function, the rate of growth of per capita income is a fixed proportion of the rate of growth of the per capita capital stock, so that the convergence parameter can be estimated within the following equation:

$$D \log y \cong \beta \log \left(\frac{y}{y^*} \right)$$

where $D\log y$ is the rate of growth of per capita income over the period, y indicates the per capita income of the ith region at the beginning of the time interval (in this case, 1980–95), y^* is the per capita income of the richest region, and β is the measure of regional convergence. The method of estimation is nonlinear least squares. In what follows I report the values of β, the convergence parameter (see table 2-4). I first look at convergence over the whole sample period and obtain a significant, but very small, convergence parameter.

Next, I consider the effect of the exchange rate regime for the convergence process, that is, whether, and to what extent, the introduction of the EMS in 1979 may have affected the regional convergence process in Europe. For this purpose, it is useful to look at three periods: the initial EMS (1980–87), the "hard EMS" (1987–92), and the period following the 1992 crisis.

The 1980–87 period, which was marked by a regime of fixed, yet adjustable exchange rates, shows no evidence of income convergence among the European regions as the parameter β is not significantly different from zero. Conversely, there appears to have been regional convergence during the period of the "hard EMS," 1987–92, which

---

27. See Barro and Sala-i-Martin (1992). This paragraph also draws on CER (1999).

TABLE 2-4. *Regional Convergence in Selected Periods*

Period	β	t value
1980–95	0.009510	5.026860
1980–87	0.001615	1.079498
1987–92	0.014207	10.21923
1992–95	−0.003343	−2.316057

SOURCE: CER (1999).

witnessed strict nominal exchange rigidity. The value of β is not significantly different from that obtained from the equation covering the
entire period. In the following period, 1992–95, which was marked by
a more flexible exchange regime and by several devaluations of currencies participating in the European exchange agreements, the opposite seems to have occurred: that is, growth rates of the European regions diverged.

The results just reported should not be overemphasized for they can
be easily explained. As regional income levels are measured at pur-
chasing power parity (PPP) exchange rates, faster income convergence
over the period of tighter monetary convergence reflects the increasing
inflation convergence among countries and regions that occurred over
that period. All the same, these results should be taken as additional
evidence of the effect of monetary integration on output convergence,
hence of partial endogeneity of another of the criteria suggested by the
optimum currency area literature, increasing similarity among regions
and thus decreasing exposure to asymmetrical shocks.

The Exchange Rate of the Euro and European Growth

The links between European economic performance and the euro's exchange rate can also be better understood by looking at the relationship between the deutsche mark and the remaining European currencies in relation to the dollar.[28] Consider, first, the comparative
evolution of real exchange rates in the United States, the European
Union as a whole, and in Germany alone.

28. This section draws on CER (1998, chap. 2).

Intra-EU Competitiveness

The period starting with the collapse of the Bretton Woods system shows a devaluation of the dollar, an essentially stable EU rate—as a period average—and the gradual real appreciation of the deutsche mark. The decline of the dollar began in 1985, immediately before the Plaza Agreements, and continued almost uninterruptedly until 1995, when a renewed strengthening of the dollar and the gradual nominal revaluation of a number of European currencies—lira, peseta, and sterling—reversed the trend.

The deutsche mark's real appreciation is thus explained partly by the dollar's movements, and partly by the wide fluctuations of real intra-European rates. Several interesting features arise here, as shown in table 2-5. Germany's intra-European competitiveness over the entire period declined by almost 20 percent, but this occurred only in the initial and final subperiods, which were characterized by the free floating of all or some of the currencies.

During the EMS period (1979–91) the real value of the deutsche mark remained stable, in fact with a slight depreciation during the years of fixed central parities (January 1987 to September 1992). The favorable trend of German competitiveness during the EMS period is explained by the real appreciation of the lira and, to a lesser degree, of the French franc, following the steady revaluation of the peseta and British pound. Moreover, from the second half of the 1980s competitiveness trends among the major European countries began to favor France, which enjoyed a greater real depreciation in 1987–91 and suffered only to a minor degree from the devaluation of the lira, peseta, and sterling following the 1992 EMS crisis.

Hence Germany has no doubt benefited from the European exchange rate agreements in the form of a clear stabilization of the real rate; besides, it is well known that the other countries have used the exchange rate as a tool for fighting inflation by accepting amounts of real appreciation and sacrificing the balance of payments target.[29] While European currencies were floating, the deutsche mark appreci-

---

29. The steady growth of Germany's favorable intra-EU trade balance during the EMS period and, conversely, the deterioration of the Italian and French balances, are dealt with in Bini Smaghi and Vona (1986).

TABLE 2-5. *Changes in Real Intra-EU Exchange Rates*

Percent

Period	Germany	France	Italy	Spain
1970–79	11.4	2.0	–13.9	–18.8
1979–87	1.8	4.6	10.3	–7.4
1987–91	–2.0	–3.3	3.2	10.1
1991–97	4.5	–1.4	–10.7	–14.9
1970–97	16.1	1.7	–12.6	–29.5
1979–97	4.2	–0.3	1.6	–13.2

SOURCE: Banca d'Italia.

ated in real terms. As a first approximation, the introduction of the single currency thus seems to shield Germany from further loss of its competitiveness with other European currencies. Although the irrevocable fixing of intra-European exchange rates is taking place under conditions of real appreciation in Germany, the same cannot be said for the other countries, whose competitiveness will probably remain unaffected (France) or improve slightly (Italy and Spain) compared with the past. Neither can the different levels of competitiveness be significantly corrected by the vanished inflation differentials.

The foregoing evidence leads to a first conclusion: under current conditions, it seems difficult to assume that the fixing of nominal exchange parities among the European currencies will lead to real disequilibria similar to those witnessed during the EMS period.[30] Despite the inclusion of the Mediterranean currencies, the euro does not seem to be affected by the original sin of replacing national currencies with unbalanced competitive situations.

The Exchange Rate and Trade in Europe

The next issue to be addressed is whether world demand and extra-EU exchange rate have had an appreciable affect on European exports for a given configuration of intra-European competitiveness. The following analysis concentrates on the specific shock factors of the non-

30. For a more detailed description, see CER (1998).

European area. Recall that intra-European exchange rate variability is often accompanied by variability with respect to third-country currencies, while the degree of synchronization of the international cycle generates an obvious correlation between Europe and the rest of the world.[31]

In order to eliminate collinearity problems, one can follow a simple econometric procedure: the real exchange rate, r, for each EU country can be regressed against a constant and a real intra-European exchange rate index.[32] Thus

$$(1) \qquad\qquad r_i = c + re_i + \varepsilon_i,$$

where re is the real intra-European exchange rate. The residual, i, of this equation has been used as an index of the real extra-EU exchange rate ($rx\varepsilon_i$):

$$(2) \qquad\qquad \varepsilon_i = rx\varepsilon_i.$$

Note that, when constructed in this way and with least squares, the real extra-EU exchange rate is not correlated to the regressor and may therefore be used to measure competitiveness shocks originating from outside the EU area. A similar procedure is used to obtain extra-EU demand as the residual of an equation in which import demand (m) of the members of the Organization for Economic Cooperation and Development (OECD) has been regressed on a European import demand index:

$$(3) \qquad\qquad m = c + me + \phi,$$

where me represents index numbers of total European imports and mxe the extra-EU imports.

The results of this exercise are shown in table 2-6. The high value of the R^2 indicates that the proportion of world demand variability attributable to non-European specific trends is quite low. Total exports of the individual countries are thus expressed as a function of both indicators of intra-European demand and exchange rate, and of the same indicators constructed for the rest of the world. Export functions are then reestimated using the new disaggregation.

31. For example, a lira/mark depreciation may be accompanied by a lira/dollar depreciation.
32. Both exchange rate indexes are from Banca d'Italia.

TABLE 2-6. *Extra-EU Import Demand,*
1970–96[a]

Logarithms of index numbers

Constant	0.02
	(2.65)
EU imports	1.16
	(63.2)
Summary statistic	
Adjusted R^2	0.99
Standard error of the regression	0.031
Durbin-Watson statistic	0.84
F statistic	3.991

a. Dependent variable is total OECD imports.
t statistics are in parentheses.

These results are reported in table 2-7. The importance of the real exchange rate for German exports is confirmed. Not only is intra-EU exchange rate elasticity higher than for other countries, but even the extra-EU exchange rate has a higher estimated coefficient than that of the other countries, with the exception of Spain. More generally, extra-EU exchange rate elasticity is higher than that of the European Union, with the exception in this case of France. The results also confirm the importance of price-competitiveness trends with respect to the non-European area for all countries, not only for the Mediterranean economies. For the United Kingdom, on the other hand, neither of the two exchange rate indicators shows significant coefficients. There are important differences in demand elasticity. European demand elasticity is lower for Germany than for the other countries, while extra-EU demand displays significant values for Italy only.

On the whole, these results suggest that shocks originating outside the area might have asymmetrical effects. A slowing down of extra-EU imports, for example, could affect Italy more markedly than other major countries. If a weakening of extra-EU demand were to be accompanied by a weakening of the dollar, and thus by a real appreciation of the euro, Germany would also be affected significantly. Similarly, if the shocks affect only the real exchange rate and not demand, the center economy would suffer heavier consequences. This leads to

TABLE 2-7. *Estimation of Export Functions in Selected Countries: Second Specification, 1975–96[a]*

Logarithms of index numbers

Function	Germany	France	Italy	Spain	United Kingdom
Constant	4.01	3.91	2.30	3.69	0.12
	(5.06)	(3.70)	(4.44)	(3.33)	(0.42)[b]
Real intra-EU exchange rate	–0.91	–0.84	–0.48	–0.75	–0.02
	(–5.21)	(–3.68)	(–4.33)	(–3.19)	(–0.30)
Real extra-EU exchange rate	–1.41	–0.81	–0.86	–2.82	0.12
	(–5.41)	(–2.45)	(–2.19)	(–6.23)	(0.58)[b]
EU imports	0.88	0.95	1.00	1.36	0.76
	(32.41)	(43.49)	(42.2)	(37.38)	(29.8)
Non-EU imports	0.24	0.24	0.86	0.47	1.12
	(1.19*)	(1.18*)	(3.48)	(1.12*)	(5.49)
d_{90}	0.11				
	(4.30)				
d_{76}				–0.15	
				(–3.06)	
Summary statistic					
Adjusted R^2	0.99	0.99	0.99	0.99	0.99
Standard error of regression	0.023	0.027	0.027	0.044	0.023
Durbin-Watson statistic	1.62	0.87	1.58	1.09	1.43
F statistic	461.72	533.15	547.70	368.70	512.20

SOURCE: OECD for exports and imports, Banca d'Italia for EU exchange rates; author's calculations for extra-EU exchange rates.

a. Figures in parentheses are *t* statistics. * denotes not significant at 10 percent.

b. The coefficient is not statistically different from zero.

a further conclusion: the consequences of possible external shocks for the euro area are uncertain and can be of different types, depending on whether the affected variable is aggregate demand or the real exchange rate.

Is There an Export-led Model of Economic Growth in Europe?

Some points can now be raised about the role of exports in the growth of the European countries. For one thing, the weight assigned to the exchange rate in the authorities' objective function would need to be directly proportional to the contribution of exports to the growth process.[33] In other words, the cost associated with giving up the exchange rate would be heavier for those countries in which there is a clearly identifiable link between exports, employment, and long-term economic growth, according to the standard export-led model. Some preliminary evidence of such a link was discussed in the preceding section. I now offer some econometric tests of an export-led model whose standard equations have been estimated for the major EU countries. The results are presented in table 2-8.

Germany is the only country for which export elasticity is statistically significant as far as employment is concerned, although this is not the case if only manufacturing employment is considered. In Germany, statistically significant relations are found for gross fixed capital formation functions as well—at a 10 percent probability level—and for manufacturing productivity; in the latter case, the relation is bidirectional. The German case, then, exhibits typical features of the export-led model, according to which employment, gross fixed capital formation, and productivity are positively induced by exports, which, in turn, are affected by productivity trends.

In other countries, the estimated relations are not significant in most cases. Only Italy shows elasticities that are not statistically different from zero for the bidirectional relation between exports and productivity. These results confirm those obtained through the causality tests (see table 2-3). For most European countries, the loss of the exchange rate should not jeopardize long-term growth, which seems to depend only marginally on exports. Germany is the significant exception inasmuch as its exports seem to be a major determinant of growth. Nevertheless, this applies only to exports toward European countries, not to those directed outside the area. The impact of the German model on the euro's exchange rate would thus be limited.

European Exports and the Dollar Exchange Rate

The final exercise of this chapter is to test whether a different composition of EMU would affect export behavior, and whether the presence of the Mediterranean economies, in particular, might affect exchange

33. See Gros (1996).

TABLE 2-8. *Exports and Economic Growth in Selected Countries: Econometric Estimation, 1970–96*

Function	Germany	France	Italy	Spain	United Kingdom
Total employment					
Constant	7.80	1.50	1.97	–0.69	3.20
Total employment (–1)	0.54	0.90	0.90	0.90	0.80
Total exports	0.06	–0.009[a]	0.01[a]	–0.01[a]	–0.00[a]
Manufacturing employment					
Constant	2.60	0.19	0.86	1.30	–0.03
Manufacturing employment (–1)	0.71	0.97	0.90	0.83	1.00
Total exports	0.03[a]	–0.02[a]	–0.05[a]	0.02[a]	0.04[a]
Private gross fixed capital formation					
Constant	4.70	1.80	6.20	2.90	2.20
Investment (–1)	0.60	0.90	0.70	0.80	0.80
Total exports	0.20[b]	0.02[a]	0.10[a]	0.0[a]	1.70[a]
Total productivity					
Constant	–0.20	0.44	0.50	0.60	0.70
Total productivity (–1)	1.00	0.90	0.90	0.90	0.85
Total exports	–0.07[a]	0.03[a]	0.04[a]	0.06[a]	0.07[a]
Manufacturing productivity					
Constant	3.23	0.14	1.30	. . .	0.50
Manufacturing productivity (–1)	0.25[a]	0.43[a]	0.66	. . .	0.80
Total exports	0.27	0.35[b]	0.32	. . .	0.21[a]
Total exports					
Constant	–3.10	–4.50	–1.30	. . .	–0.75
Total exports (–1)	0.65	0.46	0.68	. . .	0.68
Manufacturing productivity	0.72	0.81	0.34	. . .	0.27

a. The null hypothesis of nonsignificance of the coefficient is rejected with a 10 percent probability.

b. The coefficient is not statistically different from zero.

rate elasticities. The various possibilities are analyzed by comparing the results of two aggregates: one (CORE) includes Germany and those countries whose compliance with the Maastricht parameters has never been in doubt (France, Belgium, Luxembourg, the Netherlands, Denmark, Ireland); the other (EU12) includes the Mediterranean countries' economies (Italy, Spain, Portugal, Greece), as well as the United Kingdom.[34]

I estimate the export function for extra-EU exports using EURO-STAT, a different data source from that used for the estimates discussed earlier. EUROSTAT data include export quantities disaggregated by countries of destination. I first estimate the following equation:

$$(4) \qquad x_j = c + r_j + mw + d_{95} + d_{96},$$

where j = CORE or EU12, x_j are exports, r_j is the real exchange rate, and mw is world imports including imports of developing countries; d_{95} and d_{96} are two dummies.[35]

The real exchange rate with respect to the extra-EU countries is calculated as the ratio between two producer price indexes—one internal and one external to the area—and the trend of the effective nominal exchange rate in relation to the dollar, which was chosen as external reference currency. The internal price index as well as the nominal exchange rate is weighted by the country shares in total extra-area exports. The index of U.S. producer prices is used as proxy for foreign prices.

Estimation results for the period 1980–96 are shown in table 2-9. All coefficients are statistically significant and the signs are as expected. The independent variable "real exchange rate" shows a higher coefficient in the EU12 equation than in the CORE equation; in both, the elasticity of world demand is higher than that of the real exchange rate.

The lower real exchange rate elasticity found in the CORE equation is not fully consistent with the results discussed in the previous paragraphs. A different specification was therefore tested. Given the importance of the share of intra-European trade in the trade of the member countries, a new independent variable was introduced, the area's

34. Greece, the United Kingdom, and Denmark did not join EMU in the first wave. Exclusion of these countries from the estimates does not change the results reported below. Lack of data, on the other hand, has prevented the inclusion of Austria, Finland, and Sweden in the aggregates.

35. Austria, Sweden, and Finland became members of the European Union in 1995. Exports to these countries, previously included in the extra-EU aggregate, are now included in the intra-EU trade flows. The discontinuity in the data set was corrected by introducing the two dummies.

TABLE 2-9. *Estimation of the Extra-EU Export Function for Two Different European Aggregates: First Specification, 1980–96*[a]

Logarithms of index numbers

Function	EU12 equation	CORE equation
Constant	19.49	18.96
	(1339.23)	(1165.25)
Real exchange rate	–0.41	–0.19
	(–5.79)	(–2.33)
World demand	0.60	0.53
	(14.34)	(10.00)
d_{95}	–0.21	–0.25
	(–4.57)	(–4.79)
d_{96}	0.26	–0.29
	(5.50)	(–5.29)
Summary statistic		
R^2	0.98	0.91
Adjusted R^2	0.97	0.88
Standard error of regression	0.038	0.044
Durbin-Watson statistic	1.73	1.14

a. *t* statistics in parentheses.

internal demand, as distinct from extra-area export demand. The results of the estimation are shown in table 2-10.

The variable "internal demand" is not statistically significant in the CORE equation, but it is significant, with the expected sign, in the EU12 equation. In the new specification, the standard error is lower. In addition, the real exchange rate coefficient is very close to that of the CORE equation. Having taken into account the role of the internal market, the exchange rate elasticities in the two groups of countries are practically identical. Furthermore, the size of the coefficient is modest. This suggests that the broader the internal European market, the less that extra-European exports depend on the exchange rate, and thus the lower the incentive to use it to support demand.

The evidence presented in this section points to several conclusions. First, the euro replaces the currencies of countries whose competitive conditions are basically in equilibrium. This lowers the ex

TABLE 2-10. *Estimation of the Extra-EU Export Function for Two Different European Aggregates: Third Specification, 1980–96[a]*

Logarithms of index numbers

Function	EU12 equation	CORE equation
Constant	19.47	18.96
	(1666.79)	(1098.16)
Real exchange rate	–0.24	–0.19
	(–3.42)	(–1.69)
World demand	0.98	0.54
	(8.67)	(2.76)
Internal demand	–1.01	–0.05
	(–3.45)	(0.09)
d_{95}	–0.30	–0.26
	(–7.11)	(–3.84)
d_{96}	0.15	–0.29
	(3.33)	(–4.23)
Summary statistic		
R^2	0.99	0.91
Adjusted R^2	0.98	0.86
Standard error of regression	0.027	0.046
Durbin-Watson statistic	2.18	1.13

a. *t* statistics in parentheses.

ante cost associated with the loss of the exchange rate. Second, export exchange rate elasticity is higher in Germany than in the other countries. Hence it is not correct to assume that the Mediterranean economies exert stronger pressure to use the euro exchange rate to support competitiveness. Third, the asymmetrical effects of shocks originating outside Europe could turn out to be limited and could be relevant only in special circumstances. Rather, the impact on the euro would be unclear and, in any case, not likely to cause relevant policy conflicts within the ECB. Fourth, Germany is the only economy for which the export-led model seems to be consistent with evidence. In the other countries, giving up the exchange rate tool would not jeopardize growth, which depends only marginally on export pull. And fifth, export elasticity of the European aggregate is not significantly different for a smaller set of countries than for a wider one that includes the Mediterranean economies. From this point of view, the larger the number of countries in EMU, the smaller the propensity to use the euro's exchange rate to support competitiveness. Overall, the fear that Mediterranean economies might pressure the ECB for a real depreciation of the euro seems unfounded.

The EMS was quite a different matter. The structure underlying the European exchange rate mechanism was clearly asymmetrical: Germany's interest in limiting intra-European exchange rate fluctuations was coupled with the desire of other countries for a nominal anchor. In this respect, one might note the considerable widening of Germany's intra-European trade surplus that emerged during the EMS period. This asymmetry is no longer justified in EMU because now that inflation has been checked, the largest European countries face identical objectives, namely, to reestablish durable conditions for growth and to lower the high levels of unemployment. The preceding analyses emphasize that it is precisely the enlargement of EMU and of the single market that will facilitate the attainment of these objectives.

Long-term Macroeconomic Performance in Europe and the Euro's Exchange Rate

Two critical points emerge from the discussion thus far: an "active" euro exchange rate policy would produce limited benefits in terms of export-led growth, and the consolidation and extension of a euro currency region would produce long-term benefits for the euro. Hence the appropriate exchange rate policy for the euro is one geared toward long-term stability of the euro.

The Euro Exchange Rate in the Long Run

The nature of such a policy is best explained through the concept of "fundamental equilibrium exchange rate" (FEER), that is, the real rate at which internal equilibrium (where aggregate demand equals potential output under constant inflation) and external equilibrium (on current account) are simultaneously obtained.[36] This concept is useful

36. This concept was popularized by Williamson (1994). The "natural real exchange rate" is a similar concept; see Crouhy Veyrac and Saint Marc (1997). See also Gandolfo, Padoan, and Paladino (1990).

over the long run because it neglects the effects of real exchange rate fluctuations due to financial capital flows.

To determine the FEER level for the European Union, one must look for the characteristics of the EU's long-run macroeconomic equilibrium. As shown in figure 2-1, over the past two decades the European Union has more or less maintained an external equilibrium and an excess of private savings over investment, which has largely financed the public sector deficit. In this respect the public finances disequilibrium may be considered symmetrical to insufficient private sector demand.[37] By contrast, the United States has been characterized (figure 2-2) by a (long-run) private sector equilibrium and public sector deficit (now reabsorbed, however), financed by capital inflows.

The European Union has completed the fiscal adjustment required for EMU. The Stability and Growth Pact will ensure that the equilibrium will be maintained over time. In this scenario, the key policy target is to achieve a new macroeconomic equilibrium compatible with fiscal equilibrium. Several paths can lead the European Union to macroeconomic equilibrium, each with different implications for the euro's FEER. Assuming that the private demand gap is filled by boosting investment—the most desirable solution—internal and external equilibria would be attained at a higher level of income without affecting the euro's long-term exchange rate.[38] A second possibility, in the face of an unchanged demand gap (that is, without raising investment), would be to generate a current-account surplus. In this case, the European Union would transfer resources to the rest of the world by running a capital account deficit. In the long run, the accumulation of net foreign financial assets would appreciate the euro, thus making it possible to reabsorb the current-account surplus and attain an internal equilibrium at lower levels of income. A third possibility is that the European Union might be able to support a current-account deficit and a corresponding capital inflow at a constant exchange rate—as in

37. In this respect, see the analyses of Allsopp and Vines (1996). Muet (1997) and Fitoussi (1997) argue that the root of the problem of low European growth must be identified in the slowing of investment partially because of restrictive monetary policies. Moreover, the drop in the investment rate is responsible for the drop in potential output and for the rise in the unemployment rate.

38. Note that in recent years the EU's investment/GDP ratio has been continuously declining, which is the opposite of what happened in the United States.

the U.S. case—whenever internal savings fall short of financing domestic investment. This scenario has not materialized in general, but it is noteworthy that Germany has recently been able to rely on the deutsche mark's status as international currency to attract capital inflows to cover the needs that arose from the country's unification.[39]

The macroeconomic policy options have several implications for the euro's external value, and more generally for the outlook for the EU's economic policy. First, the fiscal adjustment required by the Maastricht Treaty and the Stability and Growth Pact gives the European Union room for macroeconomic maneuver. This room should be exploited to raise the private investment rate tangibly, which, in turn, could absorb those private resources that in recent years have been going largely into financing public sector needs. Second, such a macroeconomic policy orientation is not only consistent with the objectives of EMU monetary stability and the euro's external value, but it also supports investments to the extent that low and stable interest rates are the result of monetary and exchange rate stability. Third, in the medium run, such a policy underpins the euro's attributes as a desirable international currency for private investment and as reserve and reference currency for third countries.

To put the issue differently, it is inappropriate to use the euro's exchange rate for stimulating growth and investment. This point becomes even more relevant as the launching of EMU turns the European Union into more of a closed economy, much less dependent on exports for its growth. In addition, EMU opens up the possibility of managing interest rates with more independence from U.S. monetary conditions. This independence will be strengthened by the consolidation of the euro's financial market. Is this a realistic policy scenario? That question can be answered in part by drawing some lessons from past experience.

What Does the Past Record Tell?

Over the past two decades, monetary policies in Europe have relied on the exchange rate mechanism of the EMS, which has acted as a coordinating device.[40] Hence the behavior of the European Union in ag-

---

39. See Deutsche Bundesbank (1997).
40. Based on CER (1998, chap. 2).

gregate reflects this structure of monetary relations. Germany represents the exception. The Bundesbank has used the short-term interest rate to stabilize the rate of inflation and the real external value of the deutsche mark, and to stimulate growth.[41] In other words, the Bundesbank appears to have followed the so-called Taylor's rule in its monetary policy.[42] This rule posits that monetary authorities fix the short-term interest rate to minimize a loss function owing to the output gap and the divergence of the inflation rate from a desired value.[43]

This hypothesis was tested with the aid of a VAR model. The model shows the simultaneous and lagged relations between policy and nonpolicy variables.[44] Define a group of nonpolicy variables (NP) including the rate of growth of the consumer price index (Δp), industrial production (y), the short-term interest rate of the United States (r^*), and a group of policy variables (P), including the real bilateral exchange with the dollar (s), aggregate M3 in real terms ($m - p$), and the short-term interest rate (r). All variables are expressed as logarithms. Assume now that the NP variables respond with a lag of one period to the changes in P variables, while the latter respond instantly to changes in NP variables; assume also the following structural relations between the two groups of variables:

money demand – real monetary balances

(5) $m_t - p_t - y_t = trend - kr_r$

modified Taylor rule

(6) $r_t = r_t^* + \beta\Delta p_t + (1 - \beta)(y_t - trend) + \gamma s_t$

Phillips curve

(7) $(y_t - trend) = a\Delta p_t.$

41. See Juselius (1996); Clarida and Gertler (1996).

42. In formal terms, Taylor's rule is defined as $r = \tilde{r} + a \, (output \, gap) + (1 - a) \, (p - p^*)$, where r is the short-term interest rate and the tilde indicates average value, the output gap can be calculated with various methods, p is the rate of inflation, p^* is the programmed or desired rate of inflation, and a is a parameter that weights the two components of the loss function. See CER (1998, chap. 2).

43. Former U.S. Treasury secretary Robert Rubin has declared repeatedly that the Federal Reserve Board's monetary policy is designed to stabilize GDP growth around its trend value, consistent with a programmed level of inflation, and has referred explicitly to Taylor's rule.

44. I follow the approach developed in Juselius (1996); Bernanke and Mihov (1996); and Clarida and Gertler (1996).

TABLE 2-11. *Matrix P for Germany, January 1983 to December 1996*[a]

	r^*	Δp	y	s	$m - p$	r	d_{90}	trend
Δr^*	−0.003	−0.018	−2.739	0.020	2.745	0.004	0.212	−0.006
	(−0.421)	(−1.017)	(−2.416)	(0.421)	(2.487)	(0.240)	(2.962)	(−1.593)
$\Delta 2p$	−0.111	−0.896	−2.702	0.746	7.368	0.242	0.465	−0.023
	(−2.736)	(−8.864)	(−0.407)	(2.736)	(1.140)	(2.564)	(1.108)	(−1.086)
Δy	0.000	0.000	−0.135	−0.001	0.170	−0.001	0.012	0.000
	(0.554)	(0.271)	(−2.987)	(−0.554)	(3.856)	(−0.793)	(4.322)	(−2.759)
Δs	0.000	0.001	0.149	−0.002	−0.113	−0.001	−0.010	0.000
	(0.609)	(0.754)	(1.797)	(−0.609)	(−1.406)	(−0.494)	(−1.829)	(0.727)
$\Delta(m - p)$	0.000	0.000	−0.026	0.001	−0.006	0.000	0.000	0.000
	(−1.649)	(1.373)	(−2.435)	(1.649)	(−0.623)	(1.633)	(0.343)	(1.638)
Δr	0.031	0.045	3.669	−0.212	2.174	−0.073	0.036	−0.012
	(6.578)	(3.742)	(4.675)	(−6.578)	(2.846)	(−6.538)	(0.735)	(−4.788)

a. t statistics in parentheses.

Equation 5 is the standard money demand equation; equation 6 is a modified Taylor rule that includes the dynamics of the real bilateral exchange rate; equation 7 is a positive relationship between income and inflation; in this way, the reaction function of monetary policy is solved endogenously without imposing a policy objective ex ante.

Through VAR estimation, equations 5, 6, and 7 are imposed as cointegration relations. Estimation results of the impact matrix P for Germany and the European Union indicate the relations between the levels of variables and the changes in the short-term variables.

Consider, first, the results for Germany (table 2-11). The impact matrix P points to a short-term relation between German short-term interest rates and the levels of all lagged variables. The domestic interest rate exhibits an error-correcting mechanism (indicated by the negative coefficient of the lagged rate) and the standard relations assumed for the other variables. The results show a short-term monetary policy mechanism targeted at stabilization of the business cycle, the rate of inflation, and the exchange rate.

The sign of the coefficient associated with the exchange rate indicates that the German interest rate rises in the presence of a real dollar appreciation (lower s). In addition, there is a significantly positive relation with the U.S. interest rate. These results appear to confirm that German monetary policy has followed a "modified" Taylor rule

TABLE 2-12. *Matrix P for the European Union, January 1983 to December 1996*[a]

	r^*	Δp	y	s	$m - p$	r	d_{90}	trend
Δr^*	0.021	0.020	−2.546	0.192	1.323	−0.026	−0.005	−0.001
	(0.835)	(0.721)	(−1.462)	(0.585)	(0.941)	(−0.956)	(−0.063)	(−0.14)
$\Delta 2p$	0.485	−0.753	−16.016	−2.032	18.307	0.068	0.875	−0.034
	(4.320)	(−5.874)	(−2.014)	(−1.355)	(2.850)	(0.549)	(2.206)	(−1.938)
Δy	0.002	0.000	−0.171	−0.019	0.214	−0.004	0.007	0.000
	(3.340)	(0.624)	(−4.314)	(−2.48)	(6.697)	(−6.237)	(3.526)	(−4.816)
Δs	−0.007	0.004	0.497	−0.076	−0.047	−0.003	0.007	−0.001
	(−3.871)	(1.883)	(4.159)	(−3.38)	(−0.483)	(−1.6)	(1.219)	(−2.065)
$\Delta(m - p)$	0.000	0.000	−0.011	0.013	−0.016	0.001	−0.004	0.000
	(1.923)	(−0.324)	(−0.63)	(3.878)	(−1.076)	(1.858)	(−4.65)	(1.604)
Δr	−0.028	0.026	4.330	−0.344	0.505	−0.034	−0.113	−0.007
	(−1.852)	(1.512)	(4.052)	(−1.706)	(0.584)	(−2.06)	(−2.121)	(−3.198)

a. t statistics in parentheses.

to account for the effects of the course of monetary policy in the United States and for changes in the dollar exchange rate.

Results of the equation for the EU aggregate—defined as the sum of EU countries' variables—in table 2-12 are quite different. The short-term interest rate does not reflect any relationship with the changes in the other variables, except for the rate of growth. The hypothesis that the Taylor rule can be applied to EU monetary policy is therefore rejected. On the other hand, the hypothesis that the U.S. interest rate has no direct impact on the EU interest rate is confirmed, but the effect is explained indirectly via the German interest rate. This conclusion can be clarified, considering the results of the impact matrix estimates for the European Union for the period January 1983 to December 1986 (table 2-13), that is, the period immediately preceding the hard EMS. In this sub-period, in contrast to the preceding case, the U.S. interest rate does have a significant impact on that of the EU aggregate; moreover, the real bilateral euro-dollar exchange rate also has a significant impact. These two results disappear in more recent years, which are characterized by a greater degree of monetary integration in Europe.

Note that deeper European monetary integration, especially after 1987, shifts the management of the EU's external monetary relations—

TABLE 2-13. *Matrix P for the European Union, January 1983 to December 1986*[a]

	Δp	y	s	$m - p$	r	trend
Δr^*	0.066	–7.670	1.200	–25.313	0.140	0.096
	–0.566	(–1.053)	–1.145	(–1.075)	–0.481	–1.088
$\Delta 2p$	–1.985	31.467	–9.275	287.689	3.039	0.977
	(–4.944)	–1.316	(–2.698)	–3.724	–3.185	(–3.362)
Δy	0.007	–0.391	0.053	–1.481	–0.008	0.006
	–2.317	(–2.221)	–2.112	(–2.605)	(–1.102)	–2.579
Δs	0.001	–0.612	–0.005	–0.628	0.001	0.003
	–0.193	(–1.593)	(–0.093)	(–0.505)	–0.047	–0.703
$\Delta (m - p)$	0.000	–0.277	0.048	–0.733	0.008	0.003
	(–0.576)	(–7.996)	–9.674	(–6.549)	–5.844	–6.903
Δr	0.122	–1.055	–0.817	–2.958	–0.537	0.012
	–3.908	(–0.543)	(–2.923)	(–0.471)	(–6.919)	–0.491

a. *t* statistics are in parentheses.

particularly in relation to the dollar—increasingly onto German shoulders. Furthermore, the Bundesbank has discharged this responsibility by a partial decoupling from the U.S. interest rate and by attempting to stabilize the bilateral deutsche mark/dollar exchange rate.

To conclude, a Taylor rule—modified to account for exchange rate movements—explains fairly well the short-term behavior of the interest rate in Germany, but not in the EU aggregate. In the latter case, growing monetary integration in the framework of the European exchange agreements, especially during the hard EMS period, allows the short-term interest rate to become more independent from that of the United States and reduces the weight of the deutsche mark/dollar exchange rate. The EU's external monetary relations are thus "mediated" by German monetary policy. In the short run, the German interest rate reacted to changes in the deutsche mark/dollar exchange rate. In the long run, no significant relation is found between the levels of the German interest rate and the deutsche mark/dollar exchange rate, although such a relation does exist between the interest rate and inflation.[45]

45. These results are consistent with Henning's (1998) interpretation of the relation between European monetary integration and monetary relations between Europe and the United States, discussed next.

These results suggest that the ECB will not let its monetary conduct diverge significantly from that of the Bundesbank. Furthermore, the expansion of the euro market will reduce the influence of the dollar on the euro.[46] This does not necessarily mean that the ECB will follow a Taylor rule, but it does suggest European monetary policy, at least in the medium run, will continue to pursue stabilization of the exchange rate, particularly against the dollar. In the longer run, EMU could become "indifferent" to the level of the exchange rate because of the benefits of the greater size and closeness of the European economy and the relatively minor importance of the exchange rate as a support for growth (as discussed earlier). The indifference option could—and should—leave room for greater transatlantic monetary cooperation, although this would, of course, also depend on the attitude of the United States. Finally, in the long term, EMU's monetary policy will have to consider the role of the euro as a "global" currency in order to bring the EU's monetary and financial weight into line with that of its economy.

The Potential of the Euro Currency Region

From the foregoing discussion, it appears that a larger extension of EMU would increase the desirability of the euro as a global currency. The euro's potential in this regard can be assessed by examining the implications of closer ties with areas that are the most likely to become a part of the Euro region: the countries of Central and Eastern Europe (CEEC), the Mediterranean countries, and a more controversial case, those of Mercosur, the southern common market in Latin America. The three regions differ in their political and economic structure, internal composition, and in the relationship they are likely to have with EMU. To simplify a complex issue, it may be assumed that the long-term goal of CEEC is full integration into EMU; conversely (most) Mediterranean countries, while unlikely to become future members of EMU, would be part of an EU-centered economic space, while Mercosur might remain halfway between the euro and the dollar areas.

---

46. Similar hypotheses have been proposed by Masson and Turtelboom (1997) in their simulation analysis of the ECB's monetary policy.

CEEC

The CEEC case is easily stated. What matters is not "if" but "when." That is, the transition is already under way and the all-important factor is the timing and terms of the full admission to EMU (and to the European Union).[47] Evidence to date suggests that one important consideration is the sustainability of a fixed CEEC/euro exchange rate as a prerequisite for a "Maastricht" convergence process.[48] In this respect, the record is mixed. Although only some CEECs have managed to keep inflation below the double-digit range, one cannot rule out the possibility that in a period of three to five years most of these countries, especially those included in the first group of EU candidates, will be able to meet Maastricht-style criteria. Per capita GDP in most CEECs (with the exception of Bulgaria and, possibly Rumania as a consequence of the Kosovo crisis) is converging toward the German values, and income variability both between the group and the EU average and within the group is decreasing. In addition, cyclical correlation (in unemployment and production rates) with Germany has been increasing. Such evidence suggests that pegging these countries' currencies to the euro would (at least in part) amount to endogenous convergence toward optimum currency area requirements. Another question that would have to be settled, however, is the value at which the pegging should be established. Further evidence warns that an early pegging could be inconsistent with external equilibrium given rising wage levels.[49] Apart from macroeconomic convergence, increasing trade integration with EU countries would bolster the use of the euro as an invoicing currency, while the increasing trade specialization would bolster the benefits of trade integration with the European Union.[50]

In conclusion, most CEECs can be expected to shift, or have already shifted, from being part of a deutsche mark currency region—which they have been for the transition period following the fall of the Berlin wall—to a euro currency region, as a preliminary step toward full

47. The events following the Kosovo crisis will likely alter this process.
48. See Boone and Maurel (1998).
49. See Manzocchi and Ottaviano (1998).
50. For an analysis of trade integration of CEEC countries in the European Union, see Padoan (1997a).

EMU membership. In the medium run, countries such as Bulgaria and Bosnia (which have already chosen to do so) and Rumania (which might take up the option) could achieve membership in the currency region through currency board agreements.

Mediterranean Countries

Although economic integration between the European Union and the Mediterranean countries is likely to increase in the medium run, it is hard to imagine most of the countries in the area becoming full members of the union (with the exception of Cyprus and, less likely, Turkey). Nonetheless, Mediterranean countries will probably become part of the euro currency region, although the process will not be a linear one given the different relations between the single Mediterranean countries and the European Union and given the different weight of the factors (trade and financial) driving the use of the euro as a regional currency.[51]

Some of these factors might in fact reduce the momentum for such integration. For one thing, some of these countries are commodity (including oil) exporters and are unlikely to redenominate commodity prices from dollars to euros. For another, their external debt, especially long-term debt, is denominated in dollars. In 1995 the share of dollar debt was as high as 80 percent (in the case of Syria). Note, too, that most of the capital account payments and receipts are dollar denominated, with EU currencies often accounting for less than 10 percent. Equally important are the low competitiveness of European financial markets with respect to those in the United States and the special political ties that some Mediterranean countries (notably Egypt, Israel, and Turkey) have with the United States, which generate substantial financial assistance. This state of affairs will change only slowly, as euro financial markets become more efficient and as the European Union takes a more active leadership role in Mediterranean integration.

The potential for the use of the euro may be greater in trade relations, however. At present, EU-Mediterranean trade is denominated

---

51. Much of the evidence reported in this section is drawn from Chauffur and Stemitsiotis (1998).

largely in dollars even though it accounts for a large share of total Mediterranean trade. This is the result of the "vehicle currency effect." That is to say, when a small country trades with a large country, the currency of the latter is used for invoicing, whereas when two small countries trade, a third currency, usually the dollar, is used for invoicing for network externalities effects.[52] With the exception of trade with Germany (which is invoiced in deutsche marks) and, to a smaller extent, trade with France (which is invoiced in French francs), trade between EU and Mediterranean countries follows the pattern of trade invoicing between small countries.

The euro is bringing a marked change to this situation by replacing several small trading partners with a single large one, thereby generating a small countries/large country trading pattern and making the substitution of dollar invoicing with euro invoicing more appealing. Such an evolution is likely to be strengthened by the larger impact of the EMU macroeconomic cycle on the region's economies, which will in turn increase trade integration in a pattern similar to that of the European Union itself, as already mentioned. This will most likely increase the propensity of Mediterranean countries to peg their currencies to the euro for stabilization purposes. Euro invoicing and euro pegging will increase the share of euros in the reserve holdings of the Mediterranean countries. Caution will be in order, however, as the countries in the region adopt a large range of exchange rate regimes. The recent period of financial instability has softened the enthusiasm for exchange rate pegging, leaving room for either flexibility or monetary union. In the Mediterranean, then, competition between the euro and the dollar can be expected to persist for some time.

Mercosur

Competition is even more likely in the Mercosur case, which is particularly interesting because the region does not really belong to a dollar or a euro currency region, yet may have to choose between the two once the euro takes on a more global role. So the Mercosur case may be seen as a paradigmatic example of the implications of a bipolar monetary system. To assess the implications of EMU for Mercosur, it is

52. See Krugman (1992).

useful to draw on the European experience. Two issues are of relevance here: the role of monetary integration in providing an efficient stabilization mechanism and the co-evolution of trade and monetary integration. The EMS experience can be considered a successful experiment with a monetary coordination mechanism that was introduced to defeat inflation, and that shows monetary stabilization and trade integration can indeed proceed together.

Some of the Mercosur countries, Brazil and Argentina, like some of the Mediterranean countries, are large commodity exporters and hence may be exposed more than EU countries to asymmetric shocks. This suggests that they may be less inclined to rely on fixed exchange rates. On the other hand, the very process of Mercosur integration will strengthen other forms of trade—manufacturing and intra-industry trade—which will increase the benefits of monetary integration.

Another factor that clearly distinguishes Mercosur from the European Union is dollarization. The use of U.S. currency in the domestic Latin American economies takes the form of currency substitution and asset substitution, each of which has different implications for the choice of the external peg. Currency substitution refers to the use of the dollar as a unit of account (and therefore as a medium of exchange). If currency substitution is the prevailing pattern, then the appropriate policy is to peg the domestic currency to the dollar, as this increases domestic monetary stability. Asset substitution refers to the role of the dollar as a store of value (and therefore as an investment instrument). If asset substitution prevails, portfolio diversification is enhanced, and a flexible exchange rate may increase domestic monetary autonomy.

Trade integration, monetary stabilization, and dollarization suggest that Mercosur's major problem in deciding forms of monetary integration is the choice of the nominal anchor. This problem is made both more complex and amenable to different solutions by the euro. If the possibility of full monetary cooperation between the European Union and the United States is put aside, one can assume that euro-dollar behavior will most likely be unstable over the medium term. Such a scenario can be characterized as one of "mutual benign neglect." Consequently, the establishment of the euro might force Mercosur countries to face problematic choices.

Whatever path the euro-dollar exchange rate follows, Mercosur will have difficulty keeping a dollar peg. If the dollar appreciates in relation to the euro, Mercosur countries will gain in terms of stabilization (anti-inflation) benefits but will lose competitiveness in EU markets (including the markets of the "Euro region"). If the dollar depreciates in relation to the Euro, the opposite will hold: trade competitiveness will increase, and weaker and possibly adverse stabilization effects could ensue. Finally, larger euro-dollar volatility would most likely depress trade with the European Union and increase trade integration with the dollar area without adding to macroeconomic stabilization gains.

In all cases, the direction and possibly the intensity of the Mercosur integration process would be affected, given that the euro and the dollar regions are the two most important trading partners for Mercosur. The trade shares with the two regions would determine the relative importance of the effects. The current trade pattern indicates that Mercosur imports from and exports to the European Union are marginally larger than those to and from the United States and that trade with the European Union is somewhat more balanced, as the normalized trade deficit is negative in both cases. The deficit is smaller for EU trade, however, which implies less financial dependence on the European Union (according to 1991–96 data).[53] Such a trade pattern must be considered in the context of the increasing trade diversion between 1990–91 and 1996–97, which has hit the exports to Europe proportionally more than those to the United States. Over this period the share of exports to the European Union has decreased from 32 percent to 24 percent, while exports to the United States have only marginally decreased from about 22 to a little over 20 percent. Mercosur exports to Latin America have increased from 19.6 to 33.6 percent, and Latin American exports to Mercosur have more than doubled, from 10 to 23 percent. Imports from the European Union, however, have increased from 23.5 to 26.2 percent, imports from the United States have increased from 20.0 to 21.6 percent, and imports from other Latin America countries have increased from 27 to 29 percent. Given the still predominant currency substitution effect as far as dollarization is

53. IMF, Direction of Trade Statistics.

concerned, a weaker Euro would add monetary stabilization gains while strengthening the process of trade diversion toward deeper internal Mercosur trade integration.

An unstable euro-dollar relationship would put increasing pressures on Mercosur countries to choose a reference currency as a nominal anchor. If they traded predominantly with one of the two regions (which is not the current case), things would obviously be easier. The geography of trade patterns would, in other words, dictate macroeconomic priorities. In the longer run, the choice would increase the regional orientation of trade, strengthen the initial ties (for example, with the dollar region), and weaken the incentives to strengthen ties with the other region (the euro region). Instability in the euro-dollar exchange rate would further increase the asymmetrical regional pattern, also possibly increasing intra-Mercosur trade. In this respect, somewhat paradoxically, the establishment of EMU might increase rather than decrease the distance between the European Union and Mercosur. The choice for Mercosur countries will also depend, however, on the expected EU and U.S. policies toward macroeconomic performance and market access. Growth-oriented and open-market access policies will obviously greatly influence Mercosur's choice.

The natural choice for a reference currency, some might contend, is neither the dollar nor the euro, but both. That is, Mercosur should consider basket pegging. This option, while certainly possible and reasonable, may turn out to be difficult in practice if one assumes that, at least in the medium run, the euro-dollar exchange rate is likely to be quite unstable. On the other hand, such an option would become highly feasible if EU-U.S. cooperation develops.

The euro may have other implications for Mercosur as well. It will undoubtedly force Mercosur to make possibly painful choices about the future of its integration process, but it will also offer new opportunities. In the first place, Mercosur, like other countries and regions, will benefit from a new large area of monetary stability in terms of lower interest rates and larger and deeper financial markets to tap. Second, the presence of a new large financial area will offer new opportunities for international investment diversification. Third, for any given amount of trade with the European Union, transaction costs related to trade with EMU countries will be lower, and exchange risk will be reduced; that is, the benefits accruing to EMU members will be shared with their trading partners. From the Mercosur perspective, the establishment of a wide euro market will increase the weight of the asset substitution component of dollarization as foreign currencies, both the dollar and the euro, will be held for investment rather than for transaction purposes. This effect will become stronger as progress toward macroeconomic stabilization and financial market integration in Mercosur picks up, and it will increase the range of monetary policy options open to Mercosur. For these reasons, stronger ties with the euro will become more attractive for Mercosur countries. The euro-Mercosur relationship, however, will largely depend on the expected behavior of EMU authorities toward Mercosur. This includes financial support and possible agreements under which EMU authorities would be willing to act as lender-of-last-resort to Mercosur countries. In other words, the attractiveness of the euro region as a nominal anchor will, as in the case of trade policy, also depend on the perceived policy orientation of EMU authorities in cases of financial distress among countries belonging to the EMU region. However, it may also be reasonable to expect that, at least in the medium run, the union would give priority to geographically closer countries such as those of Central and Eastern Europe. But this can be expected to reinforce rather than weaken the effort the European Union should direct toward deeper integration with Mercosur in the form of increased trade and investment initiatives. Such a process would increase the attractiveness of the euro for Mercosur.

All the same, one cannot discount the consequences of deeper financial instability that seem to rule out intermediate forms of exchange rate regimes, such as pegging, which are likely to prove unsustainable. In the long run, and possibly in the medium run, the only feasible arrangements are flexible exchange rates or monetary unions, and in the case of Latin America the real alternative is dollarization, that is, the outright substitution of national currencies with the dollar. The interesting aspect of such a perspective is not which country will opt for dollarization rather than exchange rate flexibility, but what the U.S. attitude is going to be. As of mid-1999, U.S. officials have not rejected the perspective. The implications for U.S.-EMU relations may be relevant.[54]

Euro-Dollar Relations: An Uncertain Scenario

Euro-dollar relations can be viewed from at least two perspectives: relations during the transitional phase, with an eye on the immediate impact of EMU on the euro-dollar exchange rate; and relations over the longer term, in a bipolar monetary context. In the short to medium term, the euro-dollar relationship will remain asymmetrical. The stronger growth potential of the U.S. economy, which is reflected in the early depreciation of the euro, as well as the unchallenged global role of the dollar, suggest a leader-follower pattern of transatlantic monetary relations. To the extent that lower EU growth reflects unresolved structural problems and that the possibility for the euro to act as a global currency is contingent on the development of a euro-based financial system, the asymmetric relationship is likely to persist. Even so, an asymmetric relationship can be marked by different degrees of cooperation.

Will EU-U.S. relations be marked by more or less cooperation following the introduction of the single currency? Some might argue that a major institutional change such as the establishment of EMU and of a supranational monetary authority in Europe, not to mention the strengthening of supranational institutions such as the G-7, will increase the amount of transatlantic cooperation.[55] Others would counter that transatlantic cooperation is bound to decrease, for by necessity the European Union and the United States will be more interested in their domestic affairs and will seek more inward-looking strategies. Hence monetary and macroeconomic relations will move toward bilateralism rather than multilateralism.

To put things in a slightly different perspective, the "demand" for international cooperation will increase in the first scenario and will decrease in the second. If the first scenario prevails, however, the

54. The evidence is mixed. See, for instance, "Greenspan Supports Spread of the Dollar," *International Herald Tribune,* April 24–25, 1999; and "Summers Warns on Risks of Dollarization," *Financial Times,* March 15, 1999.

55. See the discussion in Henning (1999).

question remains whether a larger demand for cooperation will be matched by an increase in the "supply" of cooperation. In other words, will international institutions accommodate demand by adjusting to the new scenario? This point may be particularly worrying in the light of past experience, which suggests that in the international system the supply of cooperation usually falls short of demand. Of course, this need not be the case if one considers that a larger supply of cooperation does not necessarily imply stronger (or larger) international institutions but, in many cases, more flexible institutions.

The significant factor here will be U.S. reaction to a successful EMU. It should be recalled that America's first reaction to the Single Market initiative was one of suspicion, to say the least. The thought of a "Fortress Europe" fueled the fear that a stronger EU would accelerate the decline of U.S. economic (and political) power in the global system. Although the fear of a protectionist stance in Europe soon proved unfounded, it is sometimes argued that the launching of the Single Market accelerated the North American Free Trade Agreement (NAFTA) and strengthened the move toward trade regionalism. Accordingly, it could be that a single European currency would reinforce the tendency of international investors to diversify away from the dollar, thus weakening the U.S. currency and possibly increasing monetary regionalism. As discussed earlier, reactions to EMU might also give rise to (or a boost to) a dollar currency region in Latin America by reinforcing the tendencies of some countries in the region to take further steps toward full dollarization.

Would such developments strengthen or weaken cooperation in other areas, especially in trade relations? It could be argued that just as protectionist pressures mounted in the United States in the 1980s when the strong dollar appreciation hurt U.S. competitiveness, Europe might experience a similar reaction in the wake of strong euro appreciation. Paradoxically, the first part of 1999 has been marked by trade tensions between the European Union and the United States against the background of an appreciating dollar. This suggests that trade tensions are not necessarily linked to one specific direction in exchange rate movements.

In the longer run, once the two currencies gain equal weight, the $n-1$ problem will change. For one thing, it will not be as obvious as in the past that, because of the sheer economic size of its economy, the United States could substantially ignore the gyrations of the dollar. The establishment of a European economy operating with a single currency will by and large equalize the economic dimension of the two regions. As a consequence, the "neglect option" that has so far been a prerogative of the United States will be available to Europe as well. Stated differently, neither of the two regions will really be in a position to ignore the other or to simply adopt a leader-follower pattern.

At the same time, a stable euro-dollar exchange rate would greatly help transatlantic economic relations. It would be favored by all those actors involved in global activities, multinational firms, and sectors exposed to international competition. Furthermore, it would represent a major prerequisite for initiatives such as a new transatlantic marketplace. In addition, insofar as the medium term will see more of sectoral or specific rather than general issues on the transatlantic negotiating table—such as standards, property rights, market access, public procurements, and R&D cooperation—exchange rate manipulation would not be the appropriate policy response by either of the two sides.

In a symmetric structure, the "neglect" option becomes, apparently, more attractive, even though increasing integration and interdependence are likely to raise the costs of monetary instability that might arise. Here, incentives for cooperation—aimed perhaps at limiting exchange rate fluctuations—tend to increase. In addition, deeper financial interdependence and instability will call for more joint responsibility in providing global stabilization.

The Forces behind Stronger Cooperation

Deeper transatlantic integration clearly raises the costs of policy conflicts and promotes cooperation. This and the other factors favoring stronger cooperation can be divided into three groups: the gains from mutual concessions, the pressures from domestic constituencies, and the common external threats.

Mutual concessions would produce mutual gains. A more expansionary EMU macroeconomic policy stance, for instance, could redistribute the burden of global stabilization for the United States, while giving the European Union a stronger voice and role in international institutions. Before such gains could be realized, however, the European

Union would have to resolve its internal conflicts, which as of mid-1999 still represent an obstacle to the implementation of expansionary policies as well as the definition of a single voice in international fora.

Pressures from domestic constituencies for stronger cooperation or, at least, stable transatlantic relations, come from pro-free-trade groups on both sides of the Atlantic. Market forces, especially those more strongly associated with the globalization of capital markets and activities of multinational enterprises, will press to increase transatlantic economic integration. Private bodies—such as those organized around the Transatlantic Business Dialogue—push toward the establishment of tighter formal relationships and regulations. At the same time, such pressures will be probably resisted by those actors on both sides of the Atlantic who might consider further integration and openness a threat to the standard of living of their constituencies.

Common external threats are likely to come from financial instability. While contagion risks might be more successfully countered in the future, the consolidation of two major currency regions may well increase negative spillovers from financial instability and thus increase the scope for joint EU-U.S. action.

The Theory of International Cooperation

The theory of international economic relations, which suggests why international agreements are made and what conditions favor their success, offers some insight into cooperative behavior at the international level.[56] In the absence of a single dominant actor capable of playing a hegemonic role in the international system, cooperation is apparently favored by the following factors: a small number of actors, inasmuch as this reduces the propensity to free-ride and improves the prospects for penalizing such behavior; a long time horizon, which would allow actors to allocate a higher premium to future benefits from strengthened cooperation; institutions that favor the dissemination of information about the behavior of the actors involved and thus the transparency and predictability of such behavior; and the willingness of actors to adjust their preferences.

In the post-euro era, the first condition is obviously met, as is the third

56. For a review of this theory and its implications, see Padoan and Guerrieri (1989, chaps. 1 and 2).

if it is assumed that such institutions as the economic G-7 will continue to function—and perhaps even more effectively—and that international institutions such as the IMF will be strengthened.[57] Preferences will be difficult to adjust until EMU countries complete structural reforms and the European Union gains a more prominent voice in international financial institutions. Also, the number of actors needs closer attention because it calls for a review of the postwar evolution of monetary relations between Europe and the United States or, rather, of the consequences of U.S. behavior for Europe's international monetary policy options. These relations may be summarized as follows: whenever the United States has behaved "aggressively" in its macroeconomic and monetary relations with Europe, the European countries have increased the degree of monetary cooperation among themselves in order to stem such "aggressiveness." Conversely, periods of "benign" attitude on the part of the American authorities have slowed down monetary integration in Europe.[58]

Though apt, this description needs to be adapted to the post-euro phase, which represents the highest degree of European monetary cooperation thus far. Hence it might be more accurate to say that an "aggressive" U.S. attitude toward Europe would favor a European attitude of "noncooperation," and perhaps even an attempt to redirect broad factors of instability inside the European Union, while a benign attitude in the United States would tend to elicit a similar attitude in Europe.[59] This would be "tit-for-tat" behavior, which, however, could lead to more cooperation by making defection costs increasingly high.[60]

Conclusions

The long-term position of the euro in the international system remains unclear given the possibility of multiple equilibria in currency relations. Whether it will shift from a regional to a global role will depend on the extent to which the euro currency region will become the international (extra-EMU) domain of the single currency. But that will only

57. See Henning (1997). For the implications of the euro for international institutions, see Thygesen (1997).

58. See Henning (1998).

59. For further discussion of this scenario, see Benassy, Benoît, and Pisani-Ferry (1997).

60. See Axelrod (1984).

happen if there is increasing integration between EMU and non-EMU countries and if their policy preferences converge.

As this chapter has explained, both conditions can be met. The process of monetary integration in Europe, first through the European Monetary System and subsequently through EMU, seems to be endogenously fulfilling the requirements for an optimum currency area. In addition, there is little evidence to support the desirability of an "active" exchange rate policy for the euro to support EMU's competitiveness. On the contrary, the EU's major macroeconomic problem, a large investment gap, requires a stability-oriented monetary policy. Factors supporting a euro currency region would thus lead to a more satisfactory growth performance of Euroland, which would support the single currency in international markets.

Needless to say, the success of the euro as an international currency will also depend on its use by non-EMU countries. These regions of potential euro influence are Central and Eastern Europe, the Mediterranean countries, and Latin America (especially Mercosur). Each has different macroeconomic, trade, and institutional ties with the European Union and thus faces different incentives for using the euro as their key reference currency. In some cases at least—especially in Latin America—competition between the euro and the dollar is likely to develop because of the trend toward dollarization in the aftermath of the financial crisis of 1997–98.

These structural features of the euro currency region suggest that EU-U.S. monetary relations will remain asymmetric over the medium term as long as Europe is unable to return to a path of sustained growth and as long as international financial markets are dominated by U.S. banks and financial institutions. At the same time, transatlantic cooperation can be expected to proceed because of the high costs of a conflicting policy environment for both sides. Indeed, several incentives for cooperation are present: the mutual benefits from more balanced macroeconomic burden sharing, the pressures from proliberalization business groups, and the need for joint action in the face of international instability. Such incentives, if exploited, should enable both sides to manage their economic affairs more efficiently and to redesign international financial institutions to meet the growing challenges of globalization.

References

Allsopp, Chris, and David Vines. 1996. "Fiscal Policy and EMU." *National Institute Economic Review* (October).

Alogoskoufis, George, and Richard Portes. 1997. "European Monetary Union and International Currencies in a Tripolar World." In *Establishing a Central Bank: Issues in Europe and Lessons from the U.S.*, edited by J. Canzoneri, V. Grilli, and Paul R. Masson, 23–46. Cambridge University Press.

Artis, Michel, and Wen Zhang. 1995. "International Business Cycles and the ERM: Is There a European Business Cycle?" CEPR Discussion Paper 1191. London: Centre for Economic Policy Research (August).

Axelrod, R. 1984. *The Evolution of Cooperation.* New York: Basic Books.

Barro, Robert J., and Xavier Sala-i-Martin. 1992. *Economic Growth.* Cambridge, Mass.: MIT Press.

Bayoumi, Tamil, and Barry Eichengreen. 1992. "Shocking Aspects of Monetary Unification." CEPR Discussion Paper 643. London: Centre for Economic Policy Research (March).

Bénassy, Agnes, Benoît Mojon, and Jean Pisani-Ferry. 1997. "The Euro and Exchange Rate Stability." Paper prepared for the IMF–Camille Gutt Conference on EMU and the International Monetary System, Washington, D.C. (March 17–18).

Bergsten, C. Fred. 1996. *The Economics and Politics of United States International Monetary Policy.* New York: M. E. Sharpe.

_____. 1997. "The Impact of the Euro on Exchange Rates and International Policy Cooperation." Paper prepared for the IMF–Camille Gutt Conference on EMU and the International Monetary System, Washington, D.C. (March 17–18).

Bernanke, Ben S., and Ilia Mihov. 1996. "Measuring Monetary Policy." Princeton University.

Bini Smaghi, Lorenzo, and Stefano Vona. 1986. "Le tensioni commerciali nello Sme: Il ruolo delle politiche di cambio e della convergenza economica." Contributi all'analisi economica 2, Banca d'Italia (December).

Boone, Larry, and Mark Maurel. 1998. "Economic Convergence of the CEECs with the EU." CEPR Discussion Paper 2018. London: Centre for Economic Policy Research.

Center for Economic Policy Research (CEPR). 1995. *Monitoring European Integration 5: Unemployment Choices for Europe.* London.

Centro Europa Ricerche (CER). 1998. "Il Lavoro al Tempo dell'Euro." Report 3.

_____. 1999. "Crescita e Occupazione nell'Unione Monetaria Europea." Report.

Chauffur, Jean Pierre, and Loukas Stemitsiotis. 1998. *The Impact of the Euro on Mediterranean Partner Countries.* Euro Papers 24. Brussels: EC Commission (June).

Clarida, Richard, and Mark Gertler. 1996. "How the Bundesbank Conducts Monetary Policy." Working Paper 5581. Cambridge, Mass.: National Bureau of Economic Research.

Cohen, Benjamin J. 1998. *The Geography of Money.* Cornell University Press.

Collignon, Stefan 1997. *European Monetary Union, Convergence and Sustainability.* Paris: Association pour l'Union Monetaire en Europe.

Crouhy Veyrac, Louise, and Marc Saint Marc. 1997. "L'Euro Face au Dollar, Quel Taux de Change?" Paper presented at "Les Journées Internationales d'Economie Monetaire et Financière," Orléans (June 5–6).

Deutsche Bundesbank. 1997. "The Role of the Deutsche Mark as an International Investment and Reserve Currency." *Monthly Report* (April).

De Grauwe, Paul. 1992. *The Economics of Monetary Integration.* Oxford University Press.

Fantacone, Stefano. 1997. "L'Unione monetaria europea: Aspetti macroeconomici." In *L'Italia senza Europa: Il costo della non partecipazione alle politiche dell'Unione,* edited by Gianni Bonvicini, 90–115. Milan: F. Angeli.

Feldstein, Martin. 1997. "EMU and International Conflict." *Foreign Affairs* 76 (November/December): 60–73.

Fitoussi, Jean Paul. 1997. *Il Dibattito Proibito.* Bologna: Il Mulino.

Frankel, Jeffrey A., and Andrew K. Rose. 1996. "The Endogeneity of the Optimum Currency Area Criteria." Working Paper 5700. Cambridge, Mass.: National Bureau of Economic Research (August).

Gandolfo, Giancarlo, Pier Carlo Padoan, and Giovanna Paladino. 1990. "Exchange Rate Determination: Single Equation or Economy-wide Models? A Test against the Random Walk." *Journal of Banking and Finance* 14: 965–92.

Gros, Daniel. 1996. "A Reconsideration of the Optimum Currency Area Approach: The Role of External Shocks and Labour Mobility." *National Institute Economic Review* 158 (April): 108–18.

Henning, C. Randall. 1997. *Cooperating with Europe's Monetary Union.* Policy Analyses in International Economics 49. Washington D.C.: Institute for International Economics.

_____. 1998. "Systemic Conflict and Regional Monetary Integration: The Case of Europe." *International Organization* 52 (Summer): 537–73.

_____. 1999. "United States-European Union Relations after the Introduction of the Euro: Cooperation or Rivalry?" Paper prepared for the ECSA-TEPSA Project on Transatlantic Relations.

Juselius, Kurt. 1996. "An Empirical Analysis of the Changing Role of the German Bundesbank after 1983." *Oxford Bulletin of Economics and Statistics* 58 (4): 791–819.

Krugman, Paul. 1992. *Currencies and Crises.* MIT Press.

Manzocchi, Stefano, and Gianmarco Ottaviano. 1998. "Exchange Rate Performance in Transition Economies and EMU." Photocopy.

Masson, Paul R., and Bart G. Turtelboom. 1997. "Characteristics of the Euro, the Demand for Reserves and Policy Coordination under EMU." In *EMU and the International Monetary System,* edited by Paul R. Masson, Thomas H. Krueger, and Bart G. Turtelboom, 194–224. Washington, D.C.: International Monetary Fund.

Muet, Pierre Alain. 1997. "Deficit de Croissance et Chomage: Le Cout de la Non-cooperation." Notre Europe Study 1.

Padoan, Pier Carlo. 1995. "The International System and the Diversity of States and Markets." In *Balancing State Intervention*, edited by Robert Benjamin, Christian D. Neu, and David Quigley, 27–51. New York: St. Martin's.

————. 1997a. "Globalization and European Regional Integration." *Economia Internazionale* (November).

————. 1997b. "Regional Agreements as Clubs: The European Case." In *The Political Economy of Regionalism*, edited by Edward Mansfield and Helen Milner, 107–32. Columbia University Press.

————. 1999. "The Role of the Euro in the International System: A European View." Paper prepared for the ECSA-TEPSA Project on Transatlantic Relations.

Padoan, Pier Carlo, and Paolo Guerrieri, eds. 1989. *The Political Economy of European Integration*. Brighton: Wheatsheaf.

Portes, Richard, and Hélène Rey. 1998. "The Emergence of the Euro as an International Currency." *Economic Policy* 26 (April): 305–32.

Thygesen, Niels. 1997. "Relations among the IMF, the ECB, and the IMF's EMU Members." In *EMU and the International Monetary System*, edited by Paul R. Masson, Thomas H. Krueger, and Bart G. Turtelboom, 512–30. Washington, D.C.: International Monetary Fund.

Williamson, John. 1994. *Estimating Equilibrium Exchange Rates*. Washington, D.C.: Institute for International Economics (September).

Index